REACHING THE PEAK PERFORMANCE ZONE

REACHING THE PEAK PERFORMANCE ZONE

How to Motivate Yourself and Others to Excel

GERALD KUSHEL

amacom

American Management Association
New York • Atlanta • Boston • Chicago • Kansas City • San Francisco • Washington, D.C.
Brussels • Mexico City • Tokyo • Toronto

Library of Congress Cataloging-in-Publication Data

Kushel, Gerald.
    Reaching the peak performance zone : how to motivate yourself and others to excel / Gerald Kushel.
        p.   cm.
    Includes index.
    ISBN 0-8144-0222-4
    1. Employee motivation.   2. Achievement motivation.
3. Performance.   I. Title.
HF5549.5.M63K87   1994
658.3'14—dc20   94-21825
                                                                      CIP

Printing number

10 9 8 7 6 5 4 3 2 1

I dedicate this book to my family
Selma, Lynne, Joan, Jim
and especially to our newest addition,
Matthew

Contents

Preface And Acknowledgments

Over the years, as an international management consultant, I have been privileged to consult with, counsel, and train thousands of talented managers and executives from North America, Europe, and the Pacific Rim. During the course of this work, I have learned a great deal from the best of them. I have become privy to some of their most powerful and effective strategies. Most useful was their uncanny talent for systematically creating peak performance motivation in so many of their people.

I call those managers who have and apply this peak performance know-how "peak performance managers." Peak performance managers inevitably end up with whole peak performing business teams. And when they are in a position to do so (in the role of CEO, managing director, or company president) they inevitably create entire peak performing organizations.

I'll be explaining how they are reaching their peak performance zones in the pages ahead. And I will refer to many case examples and illustrations that are derived from my private consulting practice. Of course, as a matter of necessity, I have changed names and other identifying data in order to protect the confidentiality of my various clients and workshop participants. However, the examples and illustrations here accurately reflect the real peak performance managers and their peak performing workers whom I have studied and observed while gathering data for this book.

I particularly want to express special gratitude to my friend and associate Patrick Lybaert for his insightful suggestions in the early formulation of the Creating PPM system.

I also wish to note my indebtedness to the important work on achievement motivation by Dr. David McClelland of Harvard University. His pioneer study of achievement motivation wrestled with a central question: "What is it that gives some individuals the desire to achieve, while others are not interested in achieving at all?" In *Reaching the Peak Performance Zone*, I focus on an even larger question: What is it that motivates some people to strive for peak performance, while so many others seem to settle for standard performance or even less?

The Creating PPM system integrates the concepts of both peak performance and motivation. I acknowledge, with gratitude, the work of Charles A. Garfield and his study of peak performers described in his book *Peak Performers: The New Heroes of American Business* (New York: Avon, 1987). In addition, I wish to express appreciation for the landmark works of Abraham Maslow on motivation, especially his invaluable text *Motivation and Personality* (New York: Harper & Row, 1954).

I also owe a note of thanks to James Clarke Davis, vice-president of sales for Enron Access Corporation, for his encouraging and constructive comments on the early drafts of this work. In addition, I wish to thank my colleague and long-term friend Dr. Stan Friedland for his ongoing interest in and help with this project, especially his constructive critique of my early drafts of the WIIFM principle. And also thanks to Maggie Stuckey for her excellent editorial help. Finally, my deepest expression of appreciation goes to my dear wife, Selma, who for the past thirty-seven years has provided continuing support and help with so many of my projects, personal and professional.

Part I

Becoming a Peak Performance Manager

Imagine an organization in which each person, from top to bottom, is a peak performer; an organization in which doing one's best is the norm. Imagine what you could accomplish. Imagine how much fun you'd have!

In this book you will learn how you, as a manager, can make it happen. You will learn how to motivate peak performance in everyone who reports to you—and in yourself.

We know that peak performance is a product of self-motivation. We also know that lasting and consistent peak performance is the end result of a chain of actions. The first link in the chain is taking responsibility for one's own performance. The second link is finding a strong enough reason to perform at peak. The third link is developing the necessary know-how to perform at one's highest possible level in various situations.

In Part I, you will learn some of the fundamentals about peak performance. You will observe the qualities that separate peak performers from ordinary, run-of-the-mill performers. Importantly, you will learn the principles and techniques of effective thinking and thought-choice, which all peak performers use to motivate themselves in difficult situations. Finally, you will learn the basics of the Creating Peak Performance Motivation (PPM) system.

With these basics under your belt, you'll be on your way to creating an enthusiastic, winning team of self-motivated peak performers.

Chapter 1

Understanding Peak Performance

Was there ever an occasion, a special, almost magical time, when somehow you performed brilliantly, beyond even your highest expectations? Maybe it was during the heat of a game, or at a social event, or perhaps at work. That performance, by definition, was a peak performance.

At such a time, you were in what many refer to as "the zone," "the peak performance zone." In the zone, time seems to fly by, peak performance appears to come almost without effort, and, somehow, you just don't seem able to miss. It's the kind of zone that the basketball great Michael Jordan so often inhabited during those times when he made basket after basket in vital playoff games. If you've ever been in the peak performance zone, you'll remember how it felt.

> Theresa, age 34, is a peak performing sales representative. "Frankly, sometimes I surprise even myself. I don't seem to be able to miss. I close sale after sale—important ones, too, not just predictable sales. Don't ask me how I do it. I really don't know. I just do it."

Peak performance is what this book is all about: being a peak performer yourself, and helping others to be the same. Let's start by understanding precisely what peak performance means.

Consistent Peak Performance Pays Off

One important thing to understand about peak performance, at least as I use the term in this book, is that it is consistent. Almost everyone knows about, or has perhaps even witnessed, a once-in-a-lifetime exceptional performance. During wartime, for instance, there are numerous instances when a powerful shot of adrenalin caused by fear stimulates soldiers to perform prodigiously in the heat and stress of battle.

This kind of extraordinary performance may occur in sports competitions, in response to accidents or other family tragedies, or in times of natural disasters like floods or hurricanes. And of course it happens often in the business world, when people rush to meet deadlines or to complete a make-or-break project.

But even though they may be dramatic, one-shot peak performances don't count for much in business organizations. That's why isolated peak performances are not the focus of this book. In business and industry, only consistent and continuous peak performance pays off. And consistent, high payoff peak performance comes only from *self*-motivation.

Self-Motivation Leads to Consistent Peak Performance

Why is one performer moved to a peak performance level while another settles for a standard or even substandard performance? It's a question of attitude, and this comes from within.

Peak performers—those who turn in consistent, high-payoff performances day in and day out—have one thing in common. Their drive to excellence comes from inside themselves. No matter what their job—whether they are on staff, in operations, on the production line, in shipping, down on the shop floor, or in the mail room—peak performers are self-motivated.

> Cindy, age 31, is a television program director. Her boss says, "She's become a genius, but only through her own hard work. Having a steady job in the television industry is no easy task.

This industry is fiercely competitive. But Cindy is a standout. The best program director around. I recognized, early on, that I could only move her so far. In order for her to be the best, she had to drive herself. Cindy has made herself into one of the best. It's been her own inner drive that has separated her from the herd."

Standard and substandard performers can sometimes be encouraged by extrinsic motivators like promotions, raises, or threats of being fired. However, peak performers work energetically because they want to, because they relish the challenge.

Fred, age 51, is a building superintendent who immensely enjoys coming up with surprising solutions to seemingly unsolvable problems. "One time I worked three weeks trying to repair a huge boiler in one of my high-rise apartment buildings. No one, not the manufacturers, nor any of their so-called expert engineers that they sent out were able to fix it. But I did. I took it as a personal challenge. And I did it with nobody's help. I just did it."

Self-motivated performers don't depend on their managers to supply them with a reason for working at their peaks. Even when their relationship with the manager is positive, they don't have a sense of doing something just because "the boss said to."

Philip, age 37, is a cook in a Los Angeles restaurant. "Neil, my so-called boss, is a good-enough guy all right, and I'm glad he's got the job as supervisor. But to tell you the truth, in reality I'm my own boss—I just let him think he's important. Hell, I'll do a great job with him looking over me or without him looking over me. I just love great cooking. Always have."

The Four Performance Zones

Every team, company, or organization can be categorized as being in one of four possible zones: (1) the no performance zone, (2) the low performance zone, (3) the standard performance zone, and (4) the peak performance zone, as shown in Figure 1-1.

Figure 1-1. The four performance zone matrix.

Zone 2: Low Performance Zone substandard performers WIIF—M ("Me")	Zone 4: Peak Performance Zone peak performers WIIF—U ("Us")
Zone 1: No Performance Zone nonperformers WIIF—N ("No one")	Zone 2: Standard Performance Zone standard performers WIIF—C ("Company")

1. *The no performance zone.* This zone is peopled by those who are not doing much, either for themselves or for the organization. The presence of nonperformers indicates one of two things: poor hiring practices (in which case the practices should be changed immediately) or little incentive for these people to move out of their lethargic position. In that case, the organization owes these people something. It is entirely possible that with training these nonperformers can eventually become peak performers too.

2. *The low performance zone.* An organization that has most of its people in this zone is usually a sort of "country club." These substandard performers are obviously having their needs

met on the job. There is plenty of "What's in it for *me?* but they are doing very little to help the organization that pays them.

3. *The standard performance zone.* Organizations with most of their employees in the moderate performance zone will find that they are working hard for the company but at a sacrifice of fulfilling any of their own important interests. Essentially, these standard performers are extrinsically motivated. They need a great deal of supervision and continual external reinforcement. They are likely candidates for early burnout, heart attack, or other kinds of sickness. They respond primarily to external pressure rather than to internal motivation.

4. *The peak performance zone.* The ideal place for both workers and company is where both are serving each others' interests. That's to be found in the upper right-hand quadrant of Figure 1–1—the peak performance zone. In this zone, workers are self-starting performers. They are intrinsically motivated to do their best, having an amalgam of their own best interests and of those of the organization at heart. And because peak performance is so contagious "in the zone," eventually the entire organization may be in the peak performance zone.

In Figure 1–1, the two variables that form the matrix are "What's in it for me (WIIF—M)?" and "What's in it for the company (WIIF—C)?" Later on, I'll have more to say about WIIFMs. For the moment, note that where these two variables intersect, you have "What's in it for us (WIIF—U)?"—in other words, the peak performance zone.

The no performance organization is doomed to fail if it stays in that zone. The substandard performance organization needs all the help it can get. The standard performance organization can sometimes manage to just get by if it is lucky. Only the peak performance organization is destined for the highest level of success.

In the peak performance zone, everybody in it comes out ahead. Once a peak performance zone is established, the peak performers in that zone are not threatened by having the higher performance of one exceed that of the others. They enjoy teamwork and friendly competition. They know that as members of a peak performance team their own chances will come in due time. In the meantime, everyone benefits from everyone else's high performance.

Characteristics of Peak Performers

Obviously every organization would like to be in the peak performance zone and have every single team member be a peak performer. Just as obviously, many are not. I started to wonder why. Exactly what does it take to be a peak performer? What kind of personal qualities do peak performers have that standard performers lack?

Some time ago, I completed a study of 1,200 managers, executives, and workers from various settings. They had all been designated outstanding employees by their supervisors, but only 4 percent were true peak performers in every respect. A true peak performer has what I call three-dimensional success: peak performance on the job, high job satisfaction, and high personal life satisfaction as well. And very few of these 1,200 people had all three. Some didn't enjoy their work even though they were good at it. Others didn't have very satisfying personal lives.

Only fifty people (that's what 4 percent of 1,200 comes to) had full three-dimensional success. Not only were they high-performing on their jobs, but they also enjoyed a very high level of job satisfaction. On top of that, they had a very high level of personal life satisfaction as well.

Self-Responsibility Is the Key

The time I spent investigating these 1,200 people showed me many things about what makes peak performers tick. Most important of all, I found that all these four-percenters had one thing in common: They each took *total responsibility* for their job performance, their job satisfaction, and their personal life satisfaction. That is the key, that is what separates peak performers from ordinary performers: taking total, 100 percent responsibil-

Figure 1-2. Characteristics of peak and standard performers.

Peak Performers

▲ Take total responsibility for all their own job performances.
▲ Are effective thinkers (which is not necessarily the same as positive thinkers).
▲ Are self-motivated.
▲ Continually find sufficient reason to *want* to perform at peak level.
▲ Share generously and, hence, are excellent team players.
▲ Ask for peak performance mentoring from managers, when necessary.
▲ Have rich and satisfying personal *and* professional lives.

Standard Performers

▲ Don't take full responsibility, but blame other people, places, or things for their performance.
▲ Don't do much effective thinking.
▲ Tend to be extrinsically motivated.
▲ Don't really believe they are capable of performing at peak level and wouldn't want to even if they could.
▲ Are not the best team players and are not particularly generous in sharing with colleagues.
▲ Tend to overreact to their managers or other authority figures.
▲ Often have one-dimensional lives.

ity for themselves. Throughout this book we will look at the many ways this notion of *self-responsibility* makes such a critical difference in how people perform.

In Figure 1-2, you will see a summary of some of the important qualities that distinguish most peak performers from standard performers. Of course, not everyone can possess each and every one of these peak characteristics. They stand primarily as goals, as qualities that peak performers energetically strive to achieve.

Life in the Peak Performance Zone

When an athletic team is on a winning roll, the whole team tends to be operating in the peak performance zone. Success breeds more success. Championship teams such as the old New York Yankees, the Dallas Cowboys, and the Chicago Bulls are examples of whole teams that were obviously operating "in the zone."

Now imagine, if you will, an entire company in which workers at all levels—from the mail room to the boardroom— are all *self-motivated* to continuously improve their level of performance, to aspire to and achieve higher and higher levels of success. I'm talking about everyone: shipping clerks, the sweepers on the shop floor, the machine operators, the sales force, first-line supervisors, and all middle and upper levels of management. Job responsibilities on a team may differ, but each job has its own peak performance potential.

Is this really possible? Can an entire organization be motivated to achieve its highest peak performance level on the job? Absolutely! Developing an organization completely made up of nothing but peak performers, all working as a cohesive, championship team, all working enthusiastically for the common good—that is what this book is about. In the chapters ahead, you will learn how consistent peak performance can be achieved.

Chapter 2
The Self-Responsibility Imperative

By now you should have a very clear sense that the key to peak performance is *self-responsibility*. But what exactly does it mean?

It means simply that *you* decide how good you want to be, how hard you want to work, how thoroughly you want to do something, how far you want to go. Not your boss, not the shop steward, not your colleagues, not the president of the company. And when things don't work out as planned, you take responsibility for your mistakes and setbacks.

On the surface, self-responsibility seems a simple enough idea, but when we investigate we find it to be complex and profound. For when we look beneath the surface, we find other layers. We find the concept of thought choosing. As a rational person, you have the ability to *choose* your thoughts, to consciously select what you think. And we find the principle that feelings follow thoughts in a direct causal chain. These three concepts—thought choosing, feelings, and self-responsibility—are closely linked; in fact, each depends on the other.

In essence, this cause-and-effect process works this way: You choose a thought. That thought produces a feeling. And the combination of that thought and that feeling ultimately results in a specific behavior. How you *behave* in a particular situation is a function of how you *feel* in that situation, and that in turn is a function of how and what you *think* about that situation. Therefore, you are in control of what you do because you are in control of what you think. It is up to you whether you choose to accept responsibility or to pass the buck.

That is a quick overview; in this chapter you will learn more about these concepts.

Thoughts Lead to Feelings

Feelings never exist in a vacuum. That's sometimes hard to remember. Often it seems that our feelings just drop in on us from out of the sky, as if we are nothing but the victims of a condition we can do very little about. Yet that's simply not true. All our feelings—depression, anxiety, joy, vitality, and fatigue—have their roots in something we are thinking. Let me give you an example.

> Jack was in an elevator one day and felt the person behind him poking him in the back. He thought: "What a rude so-and-so!" And thinking this, he became highly irritated. So he turned around to give this so-and-so a piece of his mind—and discovered that person to be a blind man who was using his cane to orient himself. Quickly, Jack's thought about this man changed into "Oh, he's blind." Then immediately his feelings changed too: Instead of feeling irritated, he felt some compassion, some admiration, and a bit of chagrin for his mistake.

Your thoughts are the key to your existence: They determine both feelings and actions. Your feelings take place under your own skin; that is where you really live. And your performance, your behavior, is simply the tip of the iceberg, the small part of you that goes public. Since no one can actually see your thoughts or your feelings, your performance is apt to get most of the attention—especially in business. This point is so central to the self-responsibility concept that it is worth reminding yourself of it from time to time.

The Self-Responsibility Imperative

The process can be boiled down into one sentence, which I call the self-responsibility imperative:

Whenever necessary, pause and think, and then choose effective thoughts.

Every word of this sentence is important.

Whenever necessary is a way of encouraging you to be aware of what is happening. If you notice that your performance or emotional state is not what you want it to be, that's a "whenever necessary" time. Time to pause and think.

Pause and think means to stop thinking whatever it is that you are thinking, and to search for new, more useful thoughts. Picture yourself doing a computer scan of all the possible things you could think about a particular situation. Let all these ideas pass through your mental screen. The pause is a psychological one, and it can be very brief or it can last quite a while—however long it takes you to locate some useful, *effective thoughts.*

From this mental list of possibilities, you then actively, consciously choose an effective thought and put it in the forefront of your mind. Perhaps it was in the back of your mind all along, but something in your brain sabotaged your ability to get at it and make good use of it.

The Meaning of an Effective Thought

Effective thoughts can be defined as thoughts that are useful in terms of meeting a desired goal. A defective thought, by contrast, works against getting you to that goal. An effective thought is any thought that works to your advantage, that produces the emotional state and the kind of behavior you want. A thought that works. A useful, result-oriented thought that produces the performance result you are after.

Here's an example of the self-responsibility imperative in action.

Wanda, age 29, is in charge of information systems for an Oregon lumber mill. She has worked several weeks to prepare a speech for the annual stockholders' meeting, describing a new project she has designed. She believes the speech could make or break her career, and she is more than a bit nervous as she gets ready to walk up to the podium. But she has trained herself in effective thinking, and she knows what to do.

"Now is definitely not the time to feel nervous," she thinks to herself. (In other words, this is definitely a "whenever necessary" time.) So Wanda pauses for a few moments, and during the pause identifies certain thoughts to help her feel calm. Then she makes the conscious decision to focus on those effective thoughts so that she can deliver her presentation in top form. She reminds herself, for example, that she is well-informed on the subject matter of her talk, that she has the capacity to think spontaneously on her feet, that she has been through this before, and has always done well.

In this manner, Wanda proceeds to think her way into a calm, composed frame of mind. Then at the appointed moment, she strides confidently to the podium and gives an outstanding presentation.

Let's look at each segment of the imperative in detail; it's important that you fully understand it.

1. *Whenever Necessary.* Self-responsible peak performers are doggedly determined to have a sound emotional mind-set at all times and to perform at their best. Since this goal is always in their consciousness, they are keenly attuned to those times when their feelings and performance are not in keeping with this fundamental commitment.

For example, when suffering through a tedious presentation at a meeting, a self-responsible peak performer will notice what she is doing to herself. So she stops to pause and says to herself, "Wait a minute, this meeting isn't boring me. It's the fact that I'm trying so hard to listen to this tedious ego trip that's boring me half to death. But I don't have to sit here and suffer. I can sit here and enjoy just by thinking of something pleasurable. I wasn't put on this planet to suffer."

2. *Pause and Think.* Imagine that you and a friend have just driven a thousand miles to view the grandeur of the Grand Canyon at sunset, and you arrive just ten minutes before sunset. Moments before stepping out of your car, however, you become embroiled in a heated argument with your friend. Obviously, this is a "whenever necessary" time.

The sun is rapidly setting; time is clearly of the essence. Some foolish persons would continue the argument or at least continue to be upset and let the argument spoil the pleasure of the view. But no self-responsible effective thinker that I know of would ever do that. Instead, at such a moment, effective thinkers stop arguing and pause.

Here are some important things you can think about during the pause. You can think about how to balance your psychological compass. You can think about how to remind yourself that continuing to feel upset will most certainly defeat your primary objective "to enjoy life to the hilt."

You can quickly run through your various options: *Option 1:* You can continue feeling upset, and continue the argument. (You'll undoubtedly discard this option immediately as of little value.) *Option 2:* You can try to resolve the argument before the sunset. (This may be close to impossible.) *Option 3:* You can table the argument until after you've viewed and enjoyed the scene because it makes no sense to spoil the beauty you've traveled so far to see by continuing to argue now.

3. *Choose Effective Thoughts.* All self-responsible peak performers recognize, accept, and use free will. They know absolutely that they have the power to choose any thought they want, at any time and any place.

For the two friends at the rim of the Grand Canyon, Option 3 is obviously the wisest in view of the circumstances, and the one that undoubtedly would be chosen by self-responsible performers. Although options 1 and 2 might have merit in other contexts, they are not very attractive here. So you consciously, deliberately choose number 3—you decide that finishing the argument can wait. In a matter of seconds, you reject defective thoughts and choose an effective one.

The Choice Is Yours: Using Effective Thinking

Situation: The sun is setting. You're going to miss this spectacular sight if you don't immediately bring your emotions under control.

Defective thought:	"I can't calm down. It takes time. I'll never be able to do it."
Effective thought:	"I'll put a stop to my emotional upset immediately. I'll pause, calm down, and focus on the beauty of the view. I'll get to that unfinished emotional business later, after the sunset."

Let's look at another example. Say you've always been a perfectionist, and you know that at times it can be self-defeating. So you'd like to eliminate this trait. Pause for a few moments and figure out a thought that can help you to be less of a perfectionist. How about this one? "I don't need to be perfect, I just prefer to be perfect. I can, however, settle for excellence." That might lighten the pressure that you are putting on yourself just a little bit.

With this thought in mind, your feelings of tension are likely to change, and so will your behavior. You will probably no longer suffer from perfection paralysis; instead, you are likely to enjoy the energy that comes from working toward excellence, knowing that you don't *need* to perform perfectly, you merely *prefer* it.

Thinking and Rethinking Exercises

One excellent use of pausing is to figure out and break the pattern of a defective mind-set. It's your basic mind-set that determines what you see in a given situation. Try the following mind-set exercises, then check for the correct answers at the end.

1. What is another name for a policeman that begins with the letter "C"? The answer, of course, is cop. What is it that a rabbit does when it jumps forward? The answer, of course, is hop. What does one use to wipe up the floor? The answer is mop. What then is the first thing you do when you come to a green light?

_____

_____

_____

2. What is this?

_____

_____

_____

_____

_____

_____

3. Which is longer, the *brim* or the *peak* of this hat?

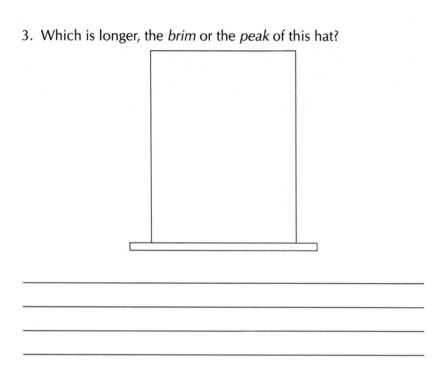

_____

_____

_____

_____

_____

_____

4. Which is correct, 8 + 9 *is* 18 or 8 + 9 *are* 18?

Answers to Mind-set Exercises

1. If you said "stop," you're wrong. That causes accidents. You must "go" at the green light.
2. A giraffe walking past a window.
3. Both are *exactly* the same length.
4. Neither: 8 + 9 = 17.

We can be duped by a self-defeating mind-set. However, in accordance with the self-responsibility imperative, we have the capacity to figure out its defect and to choose any mind-set we want, anytime or place we need to.

For example, in the Necker Cube on the next page, you can choose to see the cube projecting up *or* down depending on how you want to view it.

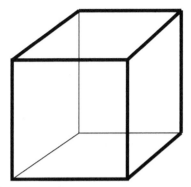

Mind-set projecting the cube upward

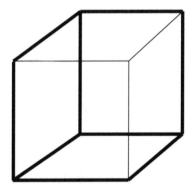

Mind-set projecting the cube downward

Much of the quality of your life depends entirely on your point of view. Look at the number 35 as it is perceived from ground level, and then as it is seen from the air. The number 35 hasn't really changed, but the different point of view certainly changes the way it appears.

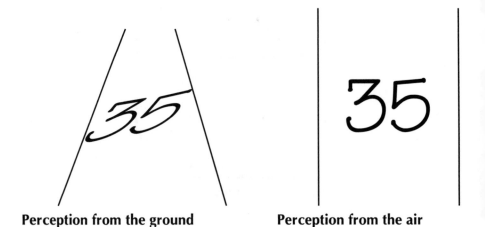

Perception from the ground   **Perception from the air**

Can You Really Choose Your Thoughts?

The self-responsibility imperative urges you to use free will in choosing effective thoughts. Some argue that there is really no such thing as free will. They contend that human beings are victims of fate or of their environment, that their capacity to choose is only an illusion. Are they right?

Often people say, "But I can't control what I think. Things just come into my head, whether I want them there or not." It is true that thoughts often seem to burst forth, appearing to rise up magically from your subconscious. But since your subconscious has been programmed, much like a computer, by parents, relatives, friends, perhaps even an enemy or two, it is prudent to be on guard. If the thoughts that happen to rise up automatically are in concert with your effective purposes, fine; but when self-defeating, defective, counterproductive thoughts rise up, thoughts that are ulcerating or insufferable, it's time to exercise your effective thinking option by *willfully* choosing thoughts that command a greater payoff. And yes, you *can* do it!

Dr. Viktor Frankl, a renowned psychiatrist, was imprisoned in Nazi concentration camps. He later wrote, "The ultimate freedom of man is the freedom to *choose* one's own attitude, regardless of external circumstances." It was through a conscious and systematic program of thought choice that Frankl enabled himself to survive the cruel and inhuman treatment given him by the Nazis. If Frankl could choose any thought he wanted in a concentration camp, we can certainly do it where we are.

You should always have at your disposal a number of thought choice options. You may not be able to act any way you want to, but you can definitely think and consequently feel any way that you want, at any time or place. This gives you tremendous personal power, since your thoughts create your feelings. The driver who hogs the highway in front of you can make you angry only if you choose anger-producing thoughts from the many thought options available to you.

Suppose, for example, the stimulus is that the vice president is yelling at you, "You're doing a terrible job in managing this department! Get this place shaped up right away!" You can mediate this stimulus simply by the thoughts you choose. Here are just a few:

Option 1: "Oh my god, I'm really destroyed. He thinks I'm terrible and my work is so important to me. I'm very upset."

Option 2: "The vice president is a fool. His remarks make him look foolish, not me."

Option 3: "The vice president is mouthing off again. I can't ever seem to please him. The hell with him. Let me focus on the more interesting aspects of life. I'll pretend that I'm very affected by his criticism, and even look ashamed. But I'll continue enjoying my life."

Option 4: "There's some truth to what the vice president is saying, even though I don't appreciate his approach. I will tighten up on managing, however. He's acting crazy. I won't take his hollering seriously. I'll show him deference, but I'll quietly make progress in my own way."

Try the following. Pause in your reading for a moment, shut your eyes, then think about something very positive, very pleasant. Remember, you can think of anything you want. It's your ultimate freedom. Why not think of something outrageous, wild, fun? You have my permission (and your own) to choose any thought at all—without charge. Perhaps you'll visualize something you never thought of before. Something that was heretofore unthinkable for you. Enjoy.

Every time I have offered this suggestion—and I've done so with hundreds of people—I have watched smiles come to many faces.

However, no matter how skilled you become at applying the self-responsibility imperative, there will be times when it is very difficult to choose a useful thought at the precise moment you want to. Instead, nasty, self-defeating thoughts sometimes rear up, spoiling your efforts. No matter how hard you try, the right thought gets squashed down by ineffective ones. When this happens, there are three other strategies you can use: I call them the A-B-C strategies, and they are explained in the next chapter.

Chapter 3
The A-B-C Method Of Thought Choice

Once you become skilled at using the self-responsibility imperative presented in Chapter 2, you will be absolutely amazed at how easily you can extricate yourself from damaging situations by changing your thoughts. However, there will inevitably be times when, no matter how hard you try, thought choosing at a conscious level just doesn't work. When that happens, you move on to *subconscious* techniques. These methods are based on what we know of human psychology; they take advantage of the amazing powers of the human mind.

The three components of the A-B-C system of thought choice are:

A = Aggravation
B = Branding
C = Closure

You should employ them in sequence, as needed. That is, if you're unsuccessful at choosing at the straightforward, conscious level, try the Aggravation Technique. If that doesn't work, you can go on to B, the Branding Tactic. If you need still more help, then move to C, the Closure Process.

A: The Aggravation Technique

The Aggravation Technique is based on the well-established psychological principle of *implosion.* Through implosion, the patient makes things worse (aggravating them) before he can make them better. For example, in order to overcome stuttering, patients are advised to deliberately stutter even more. This puts them in charge and, subsequently, often makes it easier for them to stop.

Roy, age 47, the office manager of a job search company, provides an example of how this technique can be used in the business world.

> Roy had a tendency to be rude and overbearing when he was under stress. He was disgusted with his own behavior, and he wanted to change. He tried choosing effective thoughts at the conscious level: "I feel calm. I won't get upset by minor disturbances." But it didn't work. In spite of himself, nerve-racking thoughts took over. "Feel calm," he believed, would certainly be effective if only he could choose this thought. So he decided to use the Aggravation Technique.
>
> The very next time Roy felt himself going out of control, he made himself even more nervous by choosing stress-producing thoughts: "I'm carrying too much of a work load. I get no appreciation for all the work I do. No one really cares how I feel."
>
> Having succeeded in increasing his feelings of stress, Roy was able to ask himself, "Is this the way I want to feel? *More* stressed?" And of course he answered himself, "No I don't want to feel more stressed; I want to feel calm. OK, then choose calming thoughts." By first making the situation worse, Roy was able to break through the barrier of his mental resistance; eventually he was able to choose calming thoughts.

The next time you find that you are having trouble consciously choosing productive thoughts, use the Aggravation Technique. It is especially valuable on occasions when you feel depressed for no identifiable reason and, therefore, find it difficult to locate those defective thoughts that are bringing you down. Deliberately choose thoughts that make you even more depressed; then, after you've had enough depression, you'll be ready to pause and choose thoughts about something that makes you happy. Your depression will be sure to lift because you can't feel depressed unless you actually have depression-producing thoughts preying on you.

B: The Branding Tactic

The Branding Tactic is a quick and easy *self-hypnosis* strategy that *brands* effective thoughts deeply into your subconscious. I'm going to teach you how to apply it, using the word *green.* The color green is considered by psychologists to be a very restful color, but you can use any color that you personally find soothing.

Visualize your restful color in all its natural glory. Put your conscious mind completely at ease by saying *green*, visualizing the restful beauty of the color. Take a deep breath and let your whole body relax from top to bottom.

Then say *green* again and squeeze your fingers tightly together. At this point you will bypass your conscious mind and tell yourself, "No matter how hard I try, I will not be able to separate my fingers." Be sure to go along with this suggestion and do not separate your fingers.

Now say *green* for a third time while suggesting to yourself that all the self-defeating thoughts lodged in your subconscious will fade away. Follow this with the suggestion that you will brand fully effective thoughts deeply into your subconscious. Repeat the effective thoughts (that you've prepared in advance) to yourself, several times if necessary.

Now say *green* for the fourth and last time. At this point suggest to yourself that in a few moments you will open your eyes feeling completely refreshed. Then follow your suggestion, open your eyes, and benefit from a reprogrammed subconscious.

The Branding Tactic is a quick form of self-hypnosis that can be useful to you in numerous ways: to calm yourself down quickly, to overcome such bad habits as smoking, shyness, or overeating, or just to enable you to feel more confident and enthusiastic about life. In review:

Green: "I'm completely at ease."
Green: "I can't separate my fingers, even though I try."

Green: "I'll choose the following effective thought: ____

_____

Green: "In a moment I'll open my eyes, feeling re-
             freshed, relaxed, and energized."

A + B

For weeks Sam had been troubled with insomnia; he was worried about the rash of layoffs at the factory, and his fears were
keeping him awake. As soon as Sam put the bed light out he
would think about the people who had been let go already
and about the nonstop rumors of who was going to be fired
next.

At first Sam tried the common method of counting sheep.
But nothing, not even a cup of warm milk or a hot tub before
retiring, seemed to help him fall asleep. He tried to locate
some effective thoughts to help himself, but things were just
too bad. In fact, his efforts to cease worrying at bedtime
seemed to have the opposite effect and just kept him awake.

So Sam decided to use a combination of Aggravation and
Branding. First he used the Aggravation Technique, forcing
himself to worry even more. Soon he had worked himself into
a terrible state, to the point that he realized he was actually
tired of worrying.

He then added the Branding Tactic to help him sleep. As
Sam said *green,* he felt his entire body relax completely, from
top to bottom. The moment he said *green* for the second time,
he tried to open his eyes, but to no avail. That's because he
reminded himself, "No matter how hard I try, I won't be able
to open my eyes." Of course he could actually have opened
his eyes if he had really wanted to, but he didn't because he
felt it was more important for him to have direct access to his
subconscious, the place where his basic worries resided. As
he said *green* again, Sam repeatedly chided his subconscious,
"Stop bringing all my worries home at night." He repeated this
message several times until it was deeply embedded in his
subconscious.

Then, still speaking directly to his subconscious, he said,
"You will have a series of beautiful scenes from your Vermont
vacation appear automatically in your mind in place of the

worry." He repeated this calming thought over and over again until it, too, was indelibly branded on his subconscious.

Then, with his subconscious branded (reprogrammed) to be fully effective, rather than self-defeating, he said *green* for the final time. Concurrently he said, "I will open my eyes and feel completely at ease and refreshed."

After a few moments, Sam slowly opened his eyes. For a while, he lay in bed enjoying the pleasant sensation of feeling refreshed. Then suddenly, for no obvious reason, he felt very tired, very sleepy. Sam yawned, rolled over, and in a matter of moments fell off into a deep, sound sleep.

If, after using both the A and B methods, Sam were still to find it impossible to fall asleep because of worry, he has one other very powerful strategy remaining at his disposal—the Closure Process.

C: The Closure Process

The Closure Process need only be employed when it is extremely difficult to choose effective thoughts over self-defeating ones. The reason it is sometimes so difficult to get nonproductive, self-defeating thoughts out of our heads, even after we've tried and tried, is because these self-defeating thoughts are connected with some serious unfinished business that we still have to take care of.

Unfinished business, such as not having told a loved one just how much you loved her before she died, or not having told off a colleague who insulted you, or a garage mechanic who failed to repair your car completely after you paid $1,400 in charges, can really prey on your mind. Very often we carry a large supply of unfinished business around with us for years and years, some of it dating from childhood.

If it's too late to say goodbye or to tell someone off because the person in question is no longer available, it's important to find a substitute for working through these unresolved issues. Therapists know that saying goodbye at the grave site or telling off an empty chair can often serve as a useful substitute for the real thing. Very often our dreams and nightmares help us complete this unfinished business indirectly.

Sometimes psychotherapy is needed to work through and completely close the doors on unfinished business, but often you can take care of much of your unfinished business yourself by using the Closure Process.

The Closure Process involves four distinct stages, first described by Dr. Elizabeth Kubler-Ross, the noted authority on loss counseling. These stages do not necessarily follow a particular sequence, so you can bypass one stage temporarily and then return to it later on. Eventually, however, all four stages must be completed.

The separate stages are *denial*, followed by *bargaining*, then *anger*, and finally *depression*. When you've completed these four stages, you arrive at closure. You have completed the unfinished business that has been holding you back, and now you can get on to productive functioning.

Here's how Stewart, age 43, put closure on the unfinished business connected with suddenly being fired from his job.

Stewart was loyal to his company for twelve years even though his job was very difficult and high-pressured. He gave it the very best he had at all times. "It was the first and only time in my life that I was actually fired from a job. And I took it very badly."

When the president called him on that Monday morning six years ago and announced, "You're fired," Stewart felt completely numb. He left the office in a daze and wandered around the city all day in a condition of total disbelief. He kept repeating to himself, "How unfair. How rotten. This can't really be happening to me. This must be happening to someone else, not me. This must be a dream, a nightmare. Maybe I'll wake up, and it'll be gone." Stewart was in Stage 1, *denial*.

After a short time, Stewart moved beyond his initial shock and denial and entered Stage 2, *bargaining*. During this stage, he bargained in his mind the various ways in which he could win his job back. "I'll work harder; they've got to give me another chance." Once he even fantasized that the president called him into his office to say he had made a mistake. Finally he came to realize that bargaining would be useless.

It was then that Stewart became very angry—Stage 3. It is always useful and healthy to get angry when you've been hurt, if you are careful not to hurt anyone else in the process. Hitting a pillow or cursing in the confines of your closed car are harmless outlets for anger, and they can be quite productive. So Stewart cursed his old boss, the people at that grinding company he had given so much to, and almost anyone at all he felt had even remotely contributed to sabotaging his career.

Once he had had enough of *anger* he moved on to Stage 4, *depression.* With all the heaviness of heart that goes with being let down, Stewart felt a great sadness. This was the effect of his anger turning inward. This heavy-hearted stage is essential if one is to bring unfinished psychological business to completion. After a short, intense period of depression, Stewart finally arrived at closure of the wound he had experienced from being summarily fired. At this point, he was able to accept the reality of being fired and moved forward to a productive job search.

Eventually, having found a new job and with perspective, Stewart said, "It's almost as if the firing incident happened to someone else. I can finally accept the fact that it really happened to me. It happened six years ago and, although I haven't forgotten, I certainly have forgiven."

If Stewart had not resolved this unfinished psychological business, it would still be preying on his mind and would make it extremely difficult for him to enjoy his present successes. Closure always frees you to get on with the pleasures of living.

With the self-responsibility imperative and the A-B-C strategies, you now have all you need to fully understand and internalize the concept of taking total responsibility. And that is the cornerstone of peak performance—both for you as manager and for the people you manage. In Chapter 4, we look at some of the qualities and personal traits that characterize peak performance managers.

Chapter 4

Profile of Peak Performing Managers

Performing consistently at a high level is, in and of itself, a great pleasure; being able to see similar performances by those who work with and for you can be even more enjoyable. As a peak performance manager, you will have both these pleasures.

Consistent peak performance is a challenge for anyone, but it's a special challenge for managers in that a big part of their job is to motivate others to do their best. As a manager, you want to help all your people to attain the highest possible level of performance, no matter what their job is. And to do this you must create in them the necessary degree of *self-motivation* so that they will *want* to perform at their peak level, because we know that peak performance is, by definition, self-motivated.

It sounds like an impossible task: How do you motivate self-motivation? In fact, it is possible. Peak performance managers intuitively employ a system that creates peak performance motivation in their people. I have encapsulated what they do in an uncomplicated three-step procedure (see Figure 4-1). You start with "possible" peak performers. Then, using the three-step system, you upgrade them to "probable" peak performers. Not all your "possibles" will be able to accept the self-responsibility that is required of peak performers, but those who do are on their way to becoming "practicing" peak performers.

It takes special know-how to motivate peak performers. Obviously, each employee is a special and unique individual.

Figure 4-1. Three-step Creating PPM system for managers.

1. Take total responsibility for all your own job performances, then model that quality for those who report directly to you.
2. Give all your direct reports good reasons to want to perform at peak.
3. Mentor your direct reports to the point where they are clearly performing at peak, then stay out of their way.

Consequently, the best managers are sensitive to their various dispositions, personalities, and ambitions. Peak performance managers take the time to get to know their people and to learn what makes them tick. They have a range of motivational strategies that make sense according to the needs and dispositions of their performers. They tend to see themselves as helpers, not bosses. Peak performance managers do all they possibly can do to avoid developing a "please motivate me," manager-dependent performer. Yet they know when it is time to lead, when it is time to push, and, best of all, when it is time to get and stay out of the way.

Peak Performance Managers: A Closeup

Though their ranks are relatively small, peak performance managers can be found almost anywhere business is conducted—in accounting and finance offices, in engineering divisions, computer showrooms, restaurants, barbershops, theaters, medical facilities, government offices, manufacturing plants, grocery stores, dance halls, public transportation, schools, law offices, farms, and automobile repair centers. In short, just about everywhere.

They are to be found equally among men and women and among all races, creeds, and nationalities. In the United States, Europe, the Pacific Rim, everywhere. They are also to be found among both young and old managers. It is not a matter of age that makes a peak performance manager. It is, however, a matter of sufficient seasoning. Seasoning is not the product of time *spent* on the job, but of time *invested*.

And what are they like, these high-performance managers? To begin with, they are self-motivated peak performers in their own right. And they take 100 percent responsibility for their own performance. If things go wrong, they don't blame other people—and they don't blame themselves either. Instead, they face up to whatever shortcomings the performance displayed. They learn quickly from their mistakes, and they set about quietly to improve their next performance. They are extremely resilient and able to get back on track rapidly.

> Ted, age 43, is president of a computer software company. "The way I look at my life, I'm fully in charge of this world, but only from the neck up. Surely I'm not responsible for everything that is going on in this crazy mixed-up world of ours, but I am totally responsible for myself and how I think, how I feel, and how I perform."

Peak performers are not blamers. One of the most highly cherished defense mechanisms known to the human species is blaming our failures on others. Or on equipment failure. Or on "circumstances beyond my control." But fully responsible performers do not blame others for their shortcomings. They do not even blame themselves. Taking responsibility is not quite the same as blaming. Blame implies guilt. And guilt, after the fact, is useless and debilitating.

> Lillian, age 32, is the marketing and sales manager of an Atlanta computer company: "Not too long ago," she says, "the Japanese saturated our computer markets about the same time that we expanded our line. Very poor timing on our part— and, as it happened, it was largely my decision. I'm paid to make smart decisions, not dumb ones. So I made a serious error, and I quickly admitted it. I've always learned from my mistakes. I take responsibility, but I don't walk around feeling guilty. I might make mistakes every so often, but I almost never repeat them. When you can't take the heat for your mistakes, then it's time to get out."

In addition to taking total responsibility for their own performances, peak performance managers dedicate themselves to teaching the same quality to their people. All peak performance managers are masters of human motivation and specialize in producing self-motivation in their performers. They see their job as helping all of their direct reports to bring their performance up to a peak level.

> Matt, age 53, known as the best machinist in his shop, has a peak performing manager for a boss. Matt confided, "I wasn't always such a self-motivated fellow. I learned how to be this way to a large extent from my boss, Gus. You see, Gus shares my successes. He tells everybody about how great I am. He cares about me as a human being. And now I don't need Gus or anyone else to watch over me. All anybody that I work for needs to do is to watch my smoke. Sure, Gus is very clear about what he expects from me on the job. Together, we set some work targets. Some goals. Then, once we agree on these targets, he stays out of my way unless I ask for his help. And if I do, he's there in a flash."

Conventional wisdom holds that managers must have a high profile and be on the outgoing and persuasive side. But peak performance managers are, more often than not, gentle and quietly effective. They often do much of their best work unobtrusively, working quietly behind the scenes as supporters and helpers of their peak performers. They would rather that their peak performers get the glory when glory is due.

Peak performance managers recognize that most of their direct reports look upon them as "the boss," but they do all they can to have their people eventually see themselves as their own bosses. Peak performance managers are not very impressed with job titles, seeing themselves more as a combination mentor-counselor-coach than as the boss. As such, they have no need to demand respect from those who report to them; instead, they readily earn that respect. In turn, they find their direct reports genuinely earning their respect as well.

Peak performance managers often find their people saying "We did it ourselves." And they don't mind that one bit. Many of the peak performance managers I talked to said, "I can get a lot more done around here if I don't worry a whole lot about whether I get the credit or not." Peak performance managers tend to do most of their managing behind the scenes. They tend to see themselves as someone who is there "to serve peak performers" rather than as someone who receives the award, takes the plaudits, or gets the credit. It is this genuine serving attitude that counts the most with them.

In a nutshell, the goals of peak performance managers are:

▲ To learn all they can about how to motivate peak performance
▲ To take total responsibility for their own performance and to teach this modus operandi to others
▲ To help their people get a fair share of the action
▲ To understand and model self-motivation
▲ To give their people sufficient reasons to want to excel
▲ To see themselves in a service capacity dedicated to helping others perform at peak
▲ To offer special assistance to standard performers but to stay out of the way of peak performers unless they ask for help
▲ To enjoy life in the peak performance zone

Peak performance managers tend to be pragmatists and consequently employ a variety of management styles. Their main concern is that the style they use works in a specific instance. They are flexible rather than stuck, as many conventional managers are, in a single management style. They can be autocratic, slightly paternalistic, or democratic, depending on the situation, though they lean heavily toward participatory leadership more often than not.

> Lisa, age 32, vice president of merchandising for a wholesale building supply firm, says: "I can be very directive when that is called for. But I do what works best in a given situation. Generally, however, I prefer to work behind the scenes to bring out the best in my people. I see myself as their helper, not as their boss. I don't really see that my people are working *for me*. I have them working *with me*. Frankly, I see myself working *for them*."

These managers know that what motivates one performer may not motivate another. They appreciate the diversity and the individual differences among their performers and look upon these as strengths.

> Garret, 27, is the creative director of a large advertising agency: "I have to treat each one of my people as someone who is very special. Each one of them is an artist in his or her own right. And artists, as you know, have an individual way of looking at things. All individuals are special. As artists of a sort, they need plenty of room to be autonomous."

Interestingly, each and every one of the peak performance managers that I studied had experienced a major setback of one kind or another in life. And somehow, each managed to emerge from that setback stronger than ever before.

> Peter, 44, is director of strategic planning for a manufacturer of heavy equipment. "Three years ago I got fired—out of nowhere. It was quite a shock. Naturally, I was very upset. Struggled and struggled. Finally, I got a job. This one. But I'll never forget how it felt getting fired. Before that, I thought I was invincible, and I was a bit cocky with my people. Today, I'm a whole lot more humble and more caring. I'm a better manager now because of that bad, bad experience. And I'll never forget what I learned from it."

Peak performance managers are intensely loyal to their organizations.

> Kyle, age 40, is head of security for a group of investment banks: "Look, I've worked lots of places before I came here. But in every place that I worked I gave 110 percent. If a place is good enough to pay me, and if I took the job, then I owe them my very best. No two ways about it. I can't understand how some of these younger people come to work here and think the place owes them everything, and they give nothing in return. You ought to hear how they talk. One of my main jobs here, with my new people, is to show them how caring for this company can pay off, not only for the company but for themselves as well."

Peak performance managers go out of their way to help their workers get a fair share of the action. They see "shared leadership," "a shared vision," "a shared mission," "shared authority," and "shared responsibility" as much more than just company buzzwords. It's something they believe in and therefore do their best to provide for their people.

Peak performance managers have a commitment to enjoying their managerial work as much as is humanly possible even if the conditions on the job or the nature of that job do not always make that easy to do. They have a special way of enjoying themselves even when disadvantageous circumstances might drive a lesser manager to a nervous breakdown. When, for example, peak performance managers are forced to deal with a difficult person, they look upon it as a challenge and make it their business not to let this supposedly troublesome person annoy them.

A peak performance manager never accepts that he has an incurably "lazy" person working for him. Instead, he redefines this so-called lazy worker as "insufficiently motivated." Then he figures out a way to motivate this insufficiently motivated worker.

> Kent, 52, president of a multimillion-dollar international chemical conglomerate, explains: "The only time I ever had someone working for me who was truly 'lazy' was when I, myself, was insufficiently motivated to figure out how to reach him. I think that if I'm really doing my job, I can find out how to turn on even the most difficult person."

Incidentally, Kent has a national reputation for taking former convicts, former drug addicts, and high school dropouts and converting them into very productive, successful, loyal employees.

In sum, peak performance managers see their role as a simple two-part job: helping peak performers and motivating substandard and standard performers. Their primary task, as they interpret it, is to develop, help, and nourish peak performers. They're usually not psychologists by formal training, but they're pretty good practical psychologists. They are down-to-earth experts in human motivation, especially peak performance motivation.

They teach self-responsibility and they share leadership with their people. They invest their energies in helping, nourishing, and serving the peak performers they've worked so hard to develop. They are expert at creating peak performance zones, be it within a single individual or a particular work team, department, division, or even an entire company. And then they do everything possible to keep the peak performance zone fluid and operational.

They see themselves not as "presiders" over a performer but rather as "providers" for a performer. They provide all the help necessary for a performer to develop from substandard or standard to peak. And once they have a winning team of peak performers in place, they invest the bulk of their time in serving these peak performers and enjoying life "in the zone." When the magic of the peak performance zone takes over, the manager's life becomes relatively easy. In the peak performance zone, everyone is a winner.

Figure 4-2 provides a mirror-image list of what peak performance managers do and don't do on this job.

Are You Ready to Become A Peak Performance Manager?

I expect that, if you are not quite there already, becoming a full-fledged peak performance manager is a goal that sounds worthy to you. If so, you can speed up the process by using the process of visualization. In the following exercise, you will envision yourself as already being among the best of the very best of managers—a peak performance manager. Once you see yourself that way, you will have enlisted your subconscious mind to support your efforts in that direction. Invest five or ten minutes of your time right now and complete the exercise on page 39.

Figure 4-2. Peak performance managers' do's and don'ts.

Peak Performance Managers *Do*	*Peak Performance Managers* *Don't*
▲ See themselves as helpers to and motivators of their standard performers. They tend to see themselves as equal partners with their performers, not as their superiors.	▲ Seriously see themselves as bosses or as superiors to their direct reports.
▲ Take total, 100 percent responsibility for their thoughts, feelings, and performances.	▲ Blame others or external events for their thoughts, feelings, and performances.
▲ Believe that all persons are motivated by self-interest.	▲ Believe that persons will act against their own self-interests if they know what they are.
▲ Believe that the interests of the company and the interests of its workers can be highly compatible and complementary and know how to combine these two self-interests into a successful life in the peak performance zone.	▲ Believe that the interests of the company and the interests of its workers need be mutually exclusive.
▲ Know how to listen to feelings.	▲ Believe that a worker's feelings are of little importance.
▲ Everything in their power to see to it that their standard and substandard performers learn how to take total self-responsibility.	▲ Permit or condone blaming or buck passing by anyone for any reason.
▲ Their best to provide a fair share of the action to their workers.	▲ Keep all of the action for themselves
▲ Know how to successfully employ a variety of peak performance motivational strategies, especially peak performance mentoring.	▲ Stop learning all they can about how to motivate themselves and others to higher and higher levels of peak performance.

Peak Performance Managers Do	*Peak Performance Managers Don't*
▲ Know how to create, enjoy, and sustain a highly productive, profitable, and satisfying life in the peak performance zone.	▲ Intend ever to permit themselves to slip back into being conventional or average managers.

A VISUALIZATION EXERCISE: ENJOYING MANAGERIAL LIFE IN THE PEAK PERFORMANCE ZONE

Instructions: Find a quiet place and a comfortable chair. Sit down, take a deep breath, and then relax. In order to relax, simply tighten the muscles in the back of your neck, then relax them. Then take a deep breath, and as you breathe in, think "airs of relaxation in." Then hold your breath for a moment or two. Then breathe out, thinking "tension out as I breathe out." (Do this several times, right now, until you are completely relaxed.) Now read the following, very slowly, very carefully.

[*Begin here.*]

Imagine that you have entered the peak performance zone at your place of work. In this zone, all of your people are functioning in optimal fashion as self-motivated peak performers. They are doing their very best to meet their own and the organization's goals. And they are doing very very well. Each one of your performers is highly productive, loyal, and successful in his or her own right. (Pause now to imagine that both you and your performers are enjoying the pleasure of reaping the benefits of such high achievement.) Now imagine that you are visiting each of your peak performers. Visualize seeing each one. And one by one, congratulate them for the great work that they are doing. Imagine reaching out shaking the hand of each one. One at a time, pause to enjoy the smile and to sense the genuine satisfaction that shows on the face of each one of your performers. After you have finished, pause again (for at least one minute) to relish their successes.

Now imagine that you are having a gathering of all your peak performers in your office. Imagine that you are sharing with them your feelings of pride regarding their important contributions and record-breaking achievements. You say to them the following: "I'm proud of your wonderful achievements on the job. I want you to know that whenever you feel that you want some help from me, you can count on my doing my very best to provide that help for you. I aim to provide each of you with all the materials, leadership, counseling, coaching, and mentoring that you could ever possibly want. All you need to do is mention your desire and I will definitely be there with appropriate help for you. It is my job to be available to help you to continue to perform at peak."

Pause again (for at least one minute) and think over what you have said to your people.

Now imagine all of your people continuing to do their very best both for themselves and for the company. Be sure to enjoy fully the great pleasure that you take in seeing all those who work for and alongside of you performing at peak. Enjoy both the pride and the pleasure that come from finding all of your people self-motivated peak performers who turn out high-quality work. Imagine enjoying the pleasures of a professional life that is highly productive, profitable, and very satisfying for both you and all your performers. Imagine that everything that you and your peak performers touch for the rest of your lives flourishes. Yes, that's the way of life in the peak performance zone.

Now say the following to yourself: "Yes, I find that life for me in the peak performance zone is very, very pleasurable, very profitable, and highly satisfying. I am enjoying it to the full. I am enjoying the great success and the many pleasures that go along with being a peak performance manager."

Now pause once again (only thirty seconds this time) and take another very deep breath (airs of relaxation in, tension out). During this pause, repeat the following sentence to yourself over and over again: "I find that managing in the peak performance zone provides me with great pleasure and tremendous satisfaction."

[End of exercise]

Peak performance managers know how to build an organization in which each person, from top to bottom, is empowered to do his very best. Peak performance managers create environments in which peak performance prevails as the norm. Now you're ready to learn the specific and exciting details of the three-step system for creating peak performance motivation.

Part II

Building a Self-Responsible Staff

Let's review:

Peak performance managers take full responsibility for their own performance. Through self-motivation they take responsibility for directing themselves to their own highest level, and then they teach all their direct reports—who are all potential peak performers—to do the same. They enact the self-responsibility imperative in everything they do.

Once they have taught people to take total self-responsibility, these managers promote them, in their mind's eye, from "possible" peak performers to "probable" peak performers. So Step 1 of the Creating PPM system is guiding your direct reports to take 100 percent self-responsibility for their own performance.

Next, peak performance managers do all they can to give these probable peak performers sufficient reason to want to perform up to their highest potential. This is Step 2 of the system.

Finally, these probable peak performers have the opportunity to be mentored by their managers, if they request it. As mentor, the manager helps all of them to find their own special and strong reason to excel and gives very special guidance. This is Step 3.

You would be lucky indeed if the day you became a manager you inherited an entire team of people who were already self-motivated, self-responsible peak performers. But that is not likely to happen. Instead, you will probably have to help your staff understand and fully internalize the principles of self-motivation and self-responsibility.

That process of education is what this part of the book is all about. And the process starts with you.

In this section of the book we concentrate on Step 1 of the Creating PPM system. You will learn several teaching techniques that you can use to instill the importance of total self-responsibility. But first, you must make sure that you yourself exhibit self-responsibility consistently. You can't persuade your people to do something you don't do yourself.

Chapter 5

Teaching Self-Responsibility Starts With Yourself

As a manager, training your staff to take responsibility is an important piece of your job. Later on in this section, you will learn several ways to teach self-responsibility, but the best single teaching method by far is modeling.

Modeling means setting a good example. When you take total responsibility for your own performances, you are teaching this to your direct reports by your example. Taking self-responsibility in many ways is a value, and a value is more often caught than taught.

Therefore, it behooves you to take a good look at yourself. If you have the feeling that you don't fully grasp the importance of taking total responsibility for your actions, if you don't fully understand the interconnection between thoughts, feelings, and actions, and if you haven't mastered the principle of thought choosing, go back now and reread some of the chapters in Part I. Before you can teach these principles to your staff, you must thoroughly incorporate them into your own behavior.

Do You Practice What You Preach?

The worst thing you can be, from the perspective of your direct reports, is a hypocrite. You must show by all your actions—

large and small, earthshaking and ordinary—that you completely believe in and practice the idea of self-responsibility. One
good way to find out how you're doing is by taking the following self-test. It will reveal areas that you may need to brush up
on; refer back to chapters in Part I as needed.

HOW SELF-RESPONSIBLE ARE YOU?

Instructions: Encircle the number on the line that most closely approximates the extent to which you *agree* or *disagree* with each statement.

1. I take full responsibility for all my on-the-job performances.

| 1 | 2 | 3 | 4 | 5 | 6 | 7 | 8 | 9 |

disagree   agree

2. I feel that I have a fair share of the payoffs (and losses) of this company. Consequently, I feel as if I have a vested interest in helping this company to succeed.

| 1 | 2 | 3 | 4 | 5 | 6 | 7 | 8 | 9 |

disagree   agree

3. I fully appreciate the fact that I, and I alone, choose all of my thoughts.

| 1 | 2 | 3 | 4 | 5 | 6 | 7 | 8 | 9 |

disagree   agree

4. I appreciate the value of "pausing" in order to break any self-defeating mind-set that is getting in the way of my optimal performance.

| 1 | 2 | 3 | 4 | 5 | 6 | 7 | 8 | 9 |

disagree   agree

5. I understand that my emotional state is a direct result of the thoughts I choose.

| 1 | 2 | 3 | 4 | 5 | 6 | 7 | 8 | 9 |

disagree   agree

6. I know how to systematically choose, consciously and sub-consciously, if need be, effective (useful, performance-improving) thoughts.

| 1 | 2 | 3 | 4 | 5 | 6 | 7 | 8 | 9 |

disagree   agree

7. I know how to figure out a useful performance-enhancing thought whenever I want to improve my job performance.

| 1 | 2 | 3 | 4 | 5 | 6 | 7 | 8 | 9 |

disagree   agree

8. I know how to use creative negative thinking to my own advantage when conditions warrant it.

| 1 | 2 | 3 | 4 | 5 | 6 | 7 | 8 | 9 |

disagree   agree

9. I know how to use Plan C (Closure) to rapidly work through any setback or failure I might experience on the job.

| 1 | 2 | 3 | 4 | 5 | 6 | 7 | 8 | 9 |

disagree   agree

10. I know how to enhance my thought-choosing powers by using Plan A (Aggravation), making a thing seem worse so that I can use free will to make it get better.

| 1 | 2 | 3 | 4 | 5 | 6 | 7 | 8 | 9 |

disagree   agree

11. I know how to reprogram my own subconscious, if necessary, using Plan B (Branding), a form of rapid self-hypnosis.

| 1 | 2 | 3 | 4 | 5 | 6 | 7 | 8 | 9 |

disagree   agree

12. I fully appreciate the power of the self-responsibility imperative and use it whenever appropriate.

1	2	3	4	5	6	7	8	9

disagree   agree

13. I am realistic, not merely reasonable.

1	2	3	4	5	6	7	8	9

disagree   agree

14. I believe that I am, at bottom, my own boss.

1	2	3	4	5	6	7	8	9

disagree   agree

15. I aim to be a high performer for the company, but never at the
expense of any other person.

1	2	3	4	5	6	7	8	9

disagree   agree

16. I have in my mind a battery of effective thoughts that I can
choose any time I want to upgrade an aspect of my job performance.

1	2	3	4	5	6	7	8	9

disagree   agree

17. I can readily distinguish an effective (or useful) thought from
one that may be "correct" but not especially useful or effective.

1	2	3	4	5	6	7	8	9

disagree   agree

18. I fully appreciate the difference between effective positive
    thinking and unrealistic positive thinking.

| 1 | 2 | 3 | 4 | 5 | 6 | 7 | 8 | 9 |

disagree   agree

19. I am not responsible for everything that is going on in this
    world, but I do believe that I am fully responsible for my own
    job performance—every day.

| 1 | 2 | 3 | 4 | 5 | 6 | 7 | 8 | 9 |

disagree   agree

20. I am ultimately responsible for everything that is going on in
    my own head. I don't blame other persons, places, or things
    for the thoughts I choose to use.

| 1 | 2 | 3 | 4 | 5 | 6 | 7 | 8 | 9 |

disagree   agree

Scoring

Add up the numbers you have circled. The following categories
should give you an idea of how you compare with workers who
are definitely self-responsible.

If your total is between 140 and 180, welcome to the Self-
Responsible Performers Club. Membership is open to any
worker willing to give up the most insidious of all defense
mechanisms—the blaming of others or other outside factors for
one's own performance.

If your total is between 80 and 139, you can move in either
direction—toward the taking of total, 100 percent responsibility
or toward the blaming of outside factors.

Finally, if your total is less than 80, watch out. You are very
far from taking total self-responsibility. If that is the case, some

training and learning more about how to take total self-responsibility for your own performance is in order.

This is worth repeating: The single most significant thing you can do to promote self-responsibility in your people is to model it in your own behavior.

However, chances are good that under some circumstances modeling by itself won't be sufficient. To help all of your people to reach their peak, you may have to employ some of the teaching strategies discussed in the next two chapters.

Chapter 6

Hiring Self-Responsible People

Part of your function as manager involves hiring new staff members. When this happens, you have a built-in opportunity to enlarge your team of self-responsible people. Your goal is to screen out the blamers, the job candidates who do not show signs of taking total responsibility, and to hire only those people who already take a good measure of responsibility or at least show the potential for becoming self-responsible performers.

But how do you determine whether this quality is present? When you're interviewing a job applicant, you can't very well ask:

> "Who is in charge of your job performance—you or someone else?"
> "Who chooses your thoughts—you or someone else?"
> "Are you in the habit of blaming others or outside factors when your job performance falls short?"

Even though these are the very things that you most want to know about the candidate, asking such blunt questions will probably not produce truthful answers. There are better ways to find out what you need to know.

But first, let me remind you that when interviewing a candidate, you should be looking for someone who:

▲ *Rarely or never blames other people, places, or things for his own thoughts, feelings, or behavior.* The job candidate says, for example, "I looked at it this way because it seemed to make sense at the time. My performance could have been a little bit better in the following way. . . ."

▲ *Demonstrates that he is capable of taking full and independent charge of himself.* The candidate can point to examples of self-management in the realm of job performance (such as overcoming pressures on a previous job) or in dealing with personal life issues (such as mediating family discord, handling finances, or coping with difficult people).

▲ *Shows evidence of some degree of independent achievement.* The candidate can point to accomplishments such as a project completed, a skill mastered, a hobby enthusiastically pursued, or a degree earned.

▲ *Has a sufficient level of self-esteem and a healthy degree of optimism, tempered perhaps by some skepticism, but never cynicism.* "I feel pretty good about myself," might be the candidate's response to a question about how he views himself.

▲ *Can distinguish between self-blame and self-responsibility.* For instance, the job candidate says, "It may have been my fault. But I learned from the experience, and if I get another chance, here's how I would do it better. . . ."

▲ *Has a sense that, to a great extent, she can control her own destiny.* "I often make my own luck," she answers.

▲ *Has an ambitious game plan for having an outstanding personal and professional life that doesn't depend on sheer luck.* She states, "The best is yet to come. And here's how I intend to see that it does. . . ."

▲ *Has successfully overcome at least one serious setback in life.* "Yes, I've had a setback or two in my day. And I got over them. It wasn't always easy, but I'm back on my feet now.

In short, the ideal applicant:

1. Doesn't blame others.
2. Demonstrates self-management skills.
3. Demonstrates independent achievement.
4. Has positive self-esteem.

5. Doesn't blame himself.
6. Believes in controlling his own destiny.
7. Has personal and professional goals.
8. Has overcome setbacks.

Interview Guidelines

Using whatever interview style you feel most comfortable with, try to get job candidates to tell you what they intend to do to become truly outstanding workers. To help you assess the self-responsibility level of any job candidate, try asking some variation of the five broad interview questions listed below.

Make adjustments in the wording of the questions to fit the circumstances of your industry and your own personality. The numbers listed after each question indicate which of the eight criteria listed above that particular question relates to. In each case, follow up on the applicant's answer by asking for more details or by asking other leading questions related to what the candidate is talking about.

Five Useful Leading Questions

1. "Can you tell me about a setback you have experienced in your life and how you dealt with it?" (criteria 1, 5, 6, and 8)
2. "What are some of your most significant accomplishments, personally or professionally, so far? (criteria 2, 3, 4, and 5)
3. "What are your hopes and dreams for the future?" (criteria 2, 4, 5, 6, and 7)
4. "If you happen to foul up or make a mistake on the job, and you know that it is all your fault, how do you deal with this fact?" (criteria 1, 4, 5, and 8)
5. "What is the most important thing that you will need from us in order to be an outstanding performer here. (criteria 1, 4, 6, 7, and 8)

Here is a sample interview in which the interviewer uses a form of question 1, concerning setbacks.

Manager: John, your life so far sounds as if it has gone rather smoothly.

John: Yes, I've been pretty lucky.

Manager: Did you ever have any setbacks? If you think back over your life, I imagine, if you're like most of us, you have. And if you did, can you tell me about it? I'm chiefly interested in how you handle setbacks, you know, any losses. Perhaps a mistake on the job, or a personal difficulty, or the loss of a loved one, anything like that.

[Comment: *If John says that it has always been smooth sailing, be wary. Most all persons have suffered a setback at one time or another. And if John has, how did he manage to overcome it, or is that situation still weighing him down. Look for a real person who may have been set back at one time or another but who found a way to learn from that experience and then continued to move forward.*]

The following is an example of how question 2, regarding significant accomplishments, can be of value.

John: Well, I haven't done anything special.

Manager: How about a hobby or something like that?

John: Oh, I built my own house. I love carpentry work and I built my own house from start to finish.

Manager: Wow! That sounds like a real achievement. How do you feel about having done that?

John: To tell you the truth, I'm very proud. One of the best things I've ever done.

[Comment: *This is a definite achievement and the interviewer helped John to identify it and bring it into the open. John sounds as if he has a good sense of self-esteem and can be proud of his achievements. On the other hand, if he feels he has done nothing that he can truly be proud of, he may be suffering from the kind of low self-esteem that will keep him from becoming a peak performer, the kind of person you are looking to hire.*]

As a peak performance manager, it is essential that in the future you do not hire any job candidate who fails to manifest the potential for taking total self-responsibility. Of course, you still must deal with the workers you already have on hand, whether they are self-responsible types or not. Your challenge in regard to this reality is to see to it that your entire complement of workers is trained to become totally self-responsible.

In the next chapters, you will learn several ways of teaching the principles of self-responsibility and peak performance.

Chapter 7
Self-Responsibility Seminars

If your company already has "taking full self-responsibility" in place as a corporate norm, you are fortunate indeed. But if not, you've got work to do. You must immediately try to institute a first-rate in-company training program on how to take total self-responsibility, with the aim of building as quickly as possible a winning team of self-responsible peak performers from the mail room to the boardroom. Apart from modeling self-responsible behavior yourself, supporting or contributing to such a program, seminar, or workshop is the most productive thing you can do.

There are several ways of going about this. You can plan and conduct one yourself if you have the time. Or you can ask your training department (if your company has one) to conduct it. Or you can call in a qualified outside trainer/consultant.

Planning Your Seminar

If you or your training department embark upon self-responsibility training independently, here are four suggestions.

1. Become well-versed in the principles of self-responsibility and effective thinking as described in this book.

2. Make available to all participants a copy of my earlier work, *Effective Thinking for Uncommon Success* (AMACOM, 1991).

This book carefully delineates how to use effective thinking to take total self-responsibility, and can serve as a guide for the program curriculum.

3. Make sure that your workshop participants fully understand how they can empower themselves through understanding each word of the self-responsibility imperative: "Whenever necessary, pause and think and then choose effective thoughts." Point out that effective performance begins with effective thinking.

4. Be sure to use a variety of teaching techniques during the seminar. Have open discussions, question-and-answer sessions, lectures, team-building exercises, open forums on the taking of self-responsibility, group interactions, simulations and role play about the taking of self-responsibility for one's performance. Use videos, visuals, and buzz groups. Give reading assignments and risk-taking assignments. Inspire and incite. Do everything you can think of to move your performers from being "I'm not responsible for my own performance" types to mature self-responsible performers.

The Self-Responsibility Quiz

A very good way to start off the seminar is to invite all participants to take the self-responsibility test that you yourself took in Chapter 5. Make sure they know that the quiz is merely a starting point, the results of which indicate their present level of self-responsible performance. Mention that it will also serve them as a diagnostic measure of whether there are areas of their overall job performance that would benefit from attention. Finally, let them know that although taking the quiz is entirely voluntary, it will help them to get the most out of the seminar material.

To determine their scores, have everyone add up their numbers and then explain how these figures are to be interpreted. Be sure to emphasize that whatever score participants come up with is private information, unless they want to talk it over with you.

If their total was between 140 and 180, they are qualified to be unofficial members of the Self-Responsible Performers Club. Point out that membership is open to anyone willing to give up the most insidious of all defense mechanisms, blaming other people or outside factors for one's own performance.

If their total was between 80 and 139, explain that they can move in either direction—toward the taking of total, 100 percent responsibility or toward the blaming of outside factors.

Finally, if their total was less than 80, point out that this indicates that they are taking too little self-responsibility, and invite them to decide right now to make some changes.

What to Include in the Seminar

A basic topical outline for the seminar curriculum would include:

▲ The importance of thinking
▲ How thinking affects feelings
▲ How the mind works
▲ How thinking affects performance
▲ The difference between positive thinking and effective thinking
▲ The study of four-percenters
▲ The self-responsibility imperative
▲ The difference between the taking of total self-responsibility and blaming
▲ When is "whenever necessary" time
▲ Pausing and thinking
▲ Identifying and choosing effective thoughts

The details surrounding these topics are to be found in this book as well as in *Effective Thinking for Uncommon Success.*

When and Where the Seminar Should Be Conducted

It is best if the seminar is launched at a one- or two-day off-site meeting of the participants. If possible, invite a keynote speaker, someone expert at explaining the principles of peak performance motivation, to get the ball rolling. And make sure that participants understand that this training program has the full endorsement of the company's top management.

Follow-Up

It's a good idea to provide this self-responsibility seminar on a fairly regular basis. Revisiting the seminar material will serve as a reminder of these very important concepts, which may be forgotten in time. With changing circumstances, for example, it is easy to fall back into the trap of blaming others.

At the very least, there should be follow-up meetings to ensure that the concepts relating to self-responsible performance, once they have been learned, continue to be applied. You may want to arrange for short refresher classes in the cafeteria— with the company picking up the tab for lunch.

Self-Inventory Follow-Up

Once participants take the self-responsibility inventory, most become sensitized to the various areas and keenly aware of their own performances in these areas. You might point out that any area in which they rate themselves 6 or less is an area that should be looked at. Usually the very act of taking the test produces positive changes.

To reinforce these new understandings, you might want to suggest that people take the self-inventory again one or two months after the seminar, and then periodically after that. Invite them to share the results with you, but emphasize that this is voluntary. Make sure they know that you are more than willing to talk over problem areas with them and to help them plan ways of improving their performance.

Being a good teacher is an important management skill. In addition to modeling self-responsibility and conducting (or arranging for) special in-house seminars, there are other excellent ways in which you can teach your direct reports how to take self-responsibility for all their own job performances. In Chapter 8 we look at several.

Chapter 8
Other Teaching Methods

When you take on the role of teacher, you have several methods to choose from. In the long run, the best and most effective method is teaching by example: by modeling self-responsibility. But sometimes people need the extra boost of a specific educational event. Self-responsibility seminars, described in Chapter 7, are an excellent method—but not the only one.

All good managers know the value of flexibility. The worst thing you could possibly do is to have only one way of teaching self-responsibility and then expect all your people to learn equally well from that one method. As with everything else, when it comes to teaching peak performance concepts, smart managers use what works.

Learning Styles and Methods

Each one of your performers has an individual learning style—a style that is especially suited to his own unique temperament and needs. There are four basic learning styles: the theoretical, the practical, the active, and the reflective. The theoretical draws on principles and ideas. The practical draws on experience. The active makes use of activities and actions, while the reflecting takes time for pondering and deep thought. We all learn a bit differently.

Take into consideration the learning styles of your various workers before deciding on exactly what teaching technique you'll use.

For instance, some people learn best through visualization, others through hands-on experience. Some people like classroom settings, whereas others prefer one-to-one demonstrations. Some people have to try something for themselves and even make a mistake before they can internalize the lesson. Others can learn by watching their colleagues. Some absorb information better through hearing explanations in an oral presentation; others remember more easily when they read printed material. Don't make the mistake of assuming that one technique will work for everyone; have several in your repertoire ready to be put into action.

Project Learning Method

This method provides a hands-on learning experience. You should have the person identify a specific project within the company operation that he would like to undertake. Leave him to structure and deliver a completed project to you by a certain date. Then, at the agreed-upon-time, review the quality of his self-responsible activity.

Consider also having your "students" undertake a variety of projects that will highlight self-responsibility. For example, you might ask one of them to set up a competitive team-building exercise. Have her arrange for this exercise off site, and have her make all the arrangements. Self-responsible performance in such an assignment will be easy to estimate.

Other self-responsibility assignments that you might consider are:

▲ Alone, devise a means for improving the quality of our production.
▲ Alone, devise a more efficient office system.
▲ Alone, implement a new departmental policy.
▲ Alone, redesign your workstation.
▲ Head up a productivity task force.
▲ Design a procedure to make our meetings more stimulating.
▲ Alone, prepare and give a multimedia presentation on the work of our department.

▲ Make plans for improving the company's fitness and wellness center.

▲ Conduct a survey with the object of finding a better site for our expanding company.

▲ Create a new corporate logo and company motto.

▲ Revise the company's performance assessment procedures.

On-the-Job Method

Using this teaching method, you give the performer no special training or guidelines. All you say is this: "You must learn how to take greater self-responsibility. Prove that you can do it." Then you watch the performer attempt to do so, hopefully learning by trial and error. This method can work if the person's colleagues are self-responsible performers and if you are an effective model.

Cross-Training

One of the best ways to have a performer become self-responsible is to put him to work with other individuals who are already successful at being fully self-responsible performers. Many workers tend to learn more (and more comfortably) from their peers than they do from a manager. If you can successfully enlist those workers who are already self-responsible performers to help their colleagues become that way too, you will move forward rapidly.

In this approach, self-responsible performance is taught through a combination of counseling, coaching, and mentoring. Because each of these skills requires some special know-how, I will discuss them in complete detail in chapters 12 through 14.

Combining Several Techniques

Often, a combination of seminar, project learning, on-the-job training, and cross-training is the best approach. For example:

Matt, age 26, a production engineer, often resisted taking full responsibility for his work, but his manager, zeroing in on Matt for having peak performance potential, pulled out all the stops. Not only did he insist that Matt take his ongoing self-responsibility seminar; he also encouraged him to take on a self-responsible project: "Matt, how about upgrading the tool station? Make it a three-week project." He also observed Matt while he worked at production, encouraging him, little by little, to take greater responsibility for his own actions. On top of this, he had Matt team up with Brad for some cross-training. Brad was one of the best workers in the marketing division, and from him Matt picked up both marketing know-how and a clearer picture of the usefulness (to marketing) of his production work—and, most important of all, some of Brad's self-responsible personality dimensions.

The taking of full responsibility for one's thoughts, feelings, and behavior is only the first part of the equation for reaching the peak performance zone. You have to have the proper motivation to excel. And that's next.

Part III

Motivating Peak Performance

Once people learn how to take total responsibility for their own performances, they are immediately upgraded from *possible* to *probable* peak performers. They have empowered themselves to operate at practically any performance level they choose. The next step is for them to find a sufficient reason to *want* to perform at their very best—at their peak. When they find sufficient reasons to excel—and combine these with their ability to excel—there is every reason to believe they will do so.

That brings us to Step 2 of the Creating PPM system: "Give people sufficient reasons to *want* to perform at peak." Your task, as manager, is to help people find their own self-motivations and then have them commit themselves to them.

Chapter 9
The Fundamentals
Of Motivation

Human motivation rests on one fundamental principle: All people (peak performers and all others as well) are motivated, at bottom, by self-interest. It's what is called the WIIFM principle—"What's in it for me?"

Make no mistake about it, the WIIFM principle motivates everyone, even you. All your direct reports, including the very best of them, are motivated to perform only if there is something "in it" for them personally. Otherwise, don't count on them to perform.

Sounds awfully cold and Machiavellian, doesn't it? Yet even someone as wonderful and giving as Mother Teresa acts at bottom on the basis of self-interest. It's fair to assume that doing good works makes her feel good and that she believes it puts her on good terms with the Lord. For her, those are reasons enough for doing what she does. Those are her self-interests: feeling good about herself and being closer to God. Motivation by WIIFM is a major fact of life—in all aspects of life—especially in business life.

The Basics of Motivation by WIIFM

Good managers are good motivators. And to perform well as a motivator, you need to understand some of the fundamental ingredients of the psychology of motivation.

There are several variables involved in motivation: its intensity, durability, and context and the perceptions of the person being motivated. I talk about each of these in this chapter and also about another very important concept: the difference between intrinsic and extrinsic motivation. It's especially important that you understand intrinsic motivators when guiding your people toward peak performance.

Motivational Intensity

Intensity has to do with how strongly the person wants the reward. A performer can be highly motivated, mildly motivated, or only slightly motivated depending on the intensity of the WIIFM operating. If the answer to "What's in it for me?" is "something I want very much," the performer will be highly motivated. If the answer is "something I want only slightly," then that performer will be only slightly motivated.

To help you see how valuable this is, rate yourself on the following intensity of motivation scale. Ask yourself to what degree you are motivated to perform at peak on your job? What is the intensity of your motivation. You might also suggest that your direct reports try it, perhaps as part of the self-responsibility seminar (Chapter 7) or in conjunction with counseling (discussed in Chapter 13). It's the sort of exercise that can be done periodically as a review tool.

THE INTENSITY OF MOTIVATION SCALE

| High | Average | Low | No | Demotivation |

Place a check mark at the point that indicates how motivated you are to perform at peak level on your job.

Motivational Durability

Durability has to do with how long-lasting the motivation is. One thing we have learned is that motivation tends to last longer when it is reinforced only intermittently than when it is reinforced consistently. That's because intermittent rewards tend to be perceived by a performer as having more worth. And we all like to be surprised occasionally, don't we? That's because what we take for granted is generally not appreciated as much as something we cannot take for granted.

The Japanese concept of Kaizen, "continuous improvement," leads to durable motivation. Once one improvement goal is reached, another, additional small bit of improvement is put into place. Continually chasing small bits of improvement in a constant cycle of continuous improvement breeds durable motivation.

The Context of Motivation

Context has to do with the circumstances of the motivation: the time, the place, and the way in which the reward is delivered. As to timing, psychologists have taught us that the intensity and duration of a given motivation are enhanced if the reward is provided immediately after the act. This immediate reinforcement leaves no confusion in the mind of the performer about what the reward is for. However, remember that when a reinforcement is absolutely constant, a totally guaranteed reinforcement every time a particular behavior takes place, it can lose much of its effectiveness.

Context is partly a matter of the culture of a particular organization. When a certain motivator is offered in a particular corporation, it may not have the same value it has when it is offered in another place. For instance, the key to the executive washroom in some companies is meaningful; in others, it may have no meaning at all. When thinking about what motivators to consider, it is important to be familiar with the corporate culture, the values of the company, and the kinds of people who are most appreciated by this particular company.

The Perception of the Individual

People are very complex; every individual has a different history and a unique set of values and needs. What might ordinarily be perceived as a reward by one person may be viewed as having very little value or even as a punishment by another.

In addition to conscious perceptions, there are subconscious perceptions that even the performer may not be fully aware of. On top of that, an individual can perceive a given stimulus in unpredictable ways. Even a reward that the motivator thinks of as positive can be viewed by the performer as negative.

In motivation, perception becomes reality.

Positive and Negative Motivators

Reinforcers can be either positive or negative, but positive reinforcement works best. Positive reinforcers include such things as money, better working conditions, praise, paid vacations, fringe benefits, respect, prizes, and recognition.

Negative reinforcers include such things as "taking names," "kicking butt," penalties, reprimands, docking or withholding of pay, canceling vacations, removing privileges, and showing contempt for or even ignoring the performer. In one form or another, these have been used in business settings for a long time, but the trouble with negative reinforcers is that they often prove to be highly *demotivating* instead of motivating. The intention of a negative reinforcement may be to motivate someone to stop doing something (for instance, coming in late, relaxing on the job, or working too slowly or carelessly), but if not used very judiciously, it can backfire.

Demotivation is, of course, worse than no motivation whatsoever. A performer who is insufficiently motivated (but not demotivated) may do a substandard job, but if that same person is demotivated, he may do even worse than that. To be demotivated means that neither the energy nor the commitment are there to move the performer in a particular direction. In fact, with demotivation, there is the desire to move in an opposite direction, perhaps toward sabotage.

Intrinsic or Extrinsic Motivation

What many people think of when they hear the word *motivation* are things like more money, job promotions, or special perks like individual parking spaces. But all these things are what we call *extrinsic* motivators. Extrinsic means external: Someone else is dangling this particular item in front of you as a way of getting you to do something.

Intrinsic motivators, by contrast, are internal. They originate entirely from within yourself, not from anyone or anything outside. Intrinsic motivations tend to be deeper and more personal than extrinsic motivations. And self-motivations are, by definition, intrinsic.

The following motivations are likely to be intrinsic:

▲ Enjoyment of the work itself for its own sake
▲ Desire to have a "piece of the action," such as sharing visions, missions, leadership, authority, and responsibility
▲ Pride in performing excellently
▲ Need to prove some secret point to oneself
▲ Achievement of a deep-seated value (such as helping another person)
▲ Having a deep and abiding belief in the importance of the work one is doing
▲ The excitement and pleasure of a challenge
▲ Desire to exceed one's previous level of job performance (being self-competitive)

If you as a manager want to inspire your staff to peak performance, it is particularly important that you have a clear understanding of what is extrinsic and what is intrinsic. Test yourself on your understanding of the differences with the following two quizzes.

EXTRINSIC OR INTRINSIC? QUIZ 1

Which of the following statements indicate intrinsic motivation
and which extrinsic motivation? Place an *I* in front of the statements
that you believe show intrinsic motivators at work and an *E* in front
of those that seem extrinsically motivated.

1. ___ "I perform at a high level primarily because I get
   great pleasure from a job well done."
2. ___ "I enjoy this work because I get paid well for doing
   it."
3. ___ "I perform well because I find the work I am doing
   inherently interesting."
4. ___ "I perform well because I find my work meaningful."
5. ___ "I perform well because I don't want to let my team
   down."
6. ___ "I perform well because high performance is a very
   important value to me and doing well makes me
   feel good."
7. ___ "I perform well because doing so gives me the pride
   I require in order to feel good about myself."
8. ___ "I perform well primarily in order to provide for my
   family."
9. ___ "I perform well because I am afraid to do otherwise."
10. ___ "I perform well because I just like to perform well."

Scoring: Only items 1, 3, 4, 6, 7, and 10 are intrinsic motivators.
The others are extrinsic.

EXTRINSIC OR INTRINSIC? QUIZ 2

Below are twenty verbs. Which of these verbs manifest intrinsic motivation and which extrinsic motivation? *Warning:* Be careful, this is a trick question. Place an *I* after those that seem essentially intrinsic and an *E* after those that seem essentially extrinsic.

to influence	_____	to mentor	_____
to manage	_____	to command	_____
to coach	_____	to lead	_____
to lecture	_____	to suggest	_____
to preach	_____	to pull	_____
to teach	_____	to push	_____
to demand	_____	to ask	_____
to inspire	_____	to tell	_____
to manipulate	_____	to convince	_____
to control	_____	to intimidate	_____

Scoring: Actually each and every one of the verbs is fundamentally an external, extrinsic motivator. Not a single one is inherently intrinsic. (I warned you it was tricky!)

To command a performer to report for duty on the assembly line, for example, is an extrinsic motivator. But so is it extrinsic *to suggest, to influence,* or *to ask* that performer to report for duty.

Chapter 10

Using the WIIFM Principle

We learned in Chapter 9 that WIIFM—"What's in it for me?"—is a universal principle, one that is true for everyone no matter what the circumstances of their work or lives. In this chapter we are going to consider how you can make good use of this universal truth.

Motivating "Standard" Performers

It's important for you to recognize that in this book our goal is learning how to help people excel, to help them move toward peak performance. That means, to state the matter bluntly, that we are not concerned with motivating people to do *standard* work.

In your career as a manager, you will no doubt have people reporting to you who will be content with a standard performance, and you will not be able to change that. In fact, you may need to find ways to motivate some people up from a *sub*standard level, and becoming standard is as far as they can go. There are many excellent books that can help you figure out ways to motivate poor performers to improve up to an average level, but that is not our focus here.

Having said that, however, I do want to pass on a few tips that might be helpful if you have such a person on your staff. First, remember that almost everyone responds to the WIIFM of praise and recognition. There's almost always room for more of that, even for highly self-motivated performers.

Take a tip from Ken Blanchard, author of *The One Minute Manager:* Catch your worker "doing something right" for a change instead of the more common "catching her doing something wrong." And when you do, speak up with words of praise right then. Immediate recognition, if it is appropriate, will reinforce people's willingness to continue doing a good job. But be genuine—be careful not to be saccharine.

Because every person is a unique individual, each will be inspired by different WIIFMs. As the manager, you need to invest time in getting to know your staff members a bit better so that you can begin to learn what each individual really wants. This is true for all your direct reports, but it is especially true for people who have no idea what they really want. Unfortunately, there seem to be more and more persons entering the work force every day who don't themselves know what it is that they really want.

In that case, your job is to *tell* her what she ought to want. Then simply dangle in front of her the prospect of actually achieving this, and she will be motivated accordingly. Watch out, though, because it is self-defeating to have someone become more dependent on you than she is on herself. Gradually help her to figure out on her own what she really wants.

Two WIIFMs for "Standard" Performers

Here are two WIIFMs that are effective motivators for most "standard" performers.

WIIFM 1: Be Fair. Most workers tend to see their manager as a kind of parent figure. And any parent of two or more children will tell you that one of the most difficult problems there is in raising kids is sibling rivalry. That holds true for the manager with her direct reports as well. Therefore, in using WIIFM, always be fair, or at least never give the impression that you are anything but fair-minded. Your workers have a powerful desire to be treated evenhandedly. Never do anything that would suggest you are showing favoritism, preferring one worker over another. Be fair.

WIIFM 2: Be a Winner. Most people want to attach themselves to the coattails of a winner rather than to the coattails of a nonwinner or a loser. Being or at least appearing to be successful is important. Therefore, be sure you look like a winner. In fact, being perceived as a winner and then offering your workers a fair share of all the rewards can be highly motivating—to substandard and peak performers alike.

Inspiring Others to Be Responsive to You

As a manager, your basic job is to see that the right things get done. Sometimes this means guiding and developing your immediate staff, getting things done through the efforts of those who report directly to you. And sometimes it means finding a way to influence the actions of people who do not report to you—people like your colleagues (whom you do not control) and your bosses (whom you certainly do not control). If you can get these people to respond to you, you are in a better position to influence the unfolding of events. In such situations, an understanding of the WIIFM principle can be invaluable.

Two WIIFMs for Your Boss

It probably goes without saying that you can do your own job better if you have your boss's support. You can use the WIIFM principle to enhance your position with her. When your boss appreciates you, she's more likely to give you what you need to do your own job well.

All you need to do is to figure out what your boss's WIIFM is, dangle the prospect of her achieving that reward through you, and you'll be in control. What then does your boss want from you? Here are two items that are very strong WIIFMs with most bosses.

WIIFM 1: She Wants to Look Good. Your boss has her own boss to please. Therefore, if you do things that make your boss look good in the eyes of her boss, you can motivate her to appreciate you. Find a way of publicly attributing at least a part of your success to your boss's help. It is especially effective to let your boss's boss get wind of how helpful she was.

WIIFM 2: She Needs Your Loyalty. Most bosses place a high value on their staff being loyal. Bearing this WIIFM in mind, you can motivate your boss to appreciate you even further. All you need do is to project to your boss that you are totally loyal. It's not enough to *be* loyal; you must also make sure your boss knows about it.

Two WIIFMs for Your Colleagues

Often, to achieve your own plans, you need the cooperation or assistance of other workers, your colleagues. They too are motivated by their own WIIFMs, so your task is to figure out what they might want from you and then offer them the prospect of receiving that from you—and you'll be in charge. Two WIIFMs that are generally useful for motivating one's colleagues are explained here.

WIIFM 1: They Need Assistance. It is in the self-interest of your teammates to do well on the job. Therefore, if you can provide your colleagues with the kind of help they need to do well, they will love you. Be generous and sharing and you will be in charge of the relationships you have with your teammates.

WIIFM 2: They Want to Shine. Similarly, since your teammates are interested in their own success, be sure to do nothing that smacks of "raining on their parade." Never get in the way of your colleagues' own march to success. This means that if you become too visible, do too well, and move ahead, getting the promotion that they wanted, you will be perceived as doing so at their expense. They won't mind if another company steals you and makes you president. But if you become *their* president and if they sense that you stepped over one of your colleagues in the process, beware. This WIIFM is much more difficult to take advantage of than the first one, but it is something to be sensitive about.

Chapter 11

Motivating Good Performers to Be Even Better

Motivating "probable" peak performers is largely a matter of creating an environment in which they are free to motivate themselves. In such an environment, these workers are eager to look for their own WIIFMs, for the particular payoffs that will make them *want* to perform at peak. Once they do that, they simply commit themselves to those ends and choose the thoughts, feelings, and behavior that permit them to perform the way they want to.

Here's where you can really help. It's at this point that you need all the peak performance motivational know-how you possess to work on a particular person's behalf. Start helping by trying to find out what the mind-set of your probable peak performer is (an informal counseling session is a good opportunity, as shown in Chapter 13). Once you come to understand his mind-set and view of the world, you are in a position to help him to clarify just what it is that will inspire him to do his best for the company.

Reasons to Excel

To help make this crucial point clear, I'd like to use my own experience to exemplify the kinds of things that motivate self-responsible performers.

Long ago, I began to apply effective thinking to my life, and I believe that I take total self-responsibility for my performance, including my performance as an author. Here's the way I figure it: I may proceed like a turtle rather than a hare, but if I can write a respectable sentence, then I can write a paragraph. And if I can write a paragraph, I can write a chapter. And if a chapter, I can write a book.

In fact, I have written six books. Even though most of my high school English teachers, looking down from heaven, would shake their heads in amazement that I could write even one publishable sentence, I have completed six books.

What motivates me to do this? Here are some of my own WIIFMs, or motivations to excel:

▲ I still need to prove to myself that I am not as stupid as I once thought I was.
▲ I want to continue to prove both to my wife, Selma, and to my children, Joan and Lynne, that I am something special. And I want to share my ideas with them because I think these ideas will prove to be very helpful to them in their own development.
▲ Writing books makes me feel as if I am not just run-of-the-mill, and I want very much to be special.
▲ Staying home and writing keeps me from getting into trouble. It keeps me gainfully occupied, and I can work at my own pace and to my own schedule.
▲ I can't think of anything else that I can do that is more challenging, and I like challenges.
▲ I love seeing my ideas in print.
▲ I'll have something to show for my life.
▲ Being published is prestigious, and besides there is money that can be made from it. And who can't use a little more money—perhaps to give to my favorite charity?
▲ I'm a bit of an altruist, and I think my ideas are something of a gift to others.
▲ It's a way of being sure that my talks and seminars (which I love to give) are on the cutting edge. Writing keeps me sharp and in touch with fresh ideas.

Intrinsic Motivators for Peak Performers

The WIIFMs for self-responsible performers are usually quite different from those that motivate performers who function at a standard or lower performance level. Since self-responsible performers tend to march to their own drummer, the kinds of WIIFMs that will move such people are likely to be intrinsic rather than extrinsic.

But with peak performers or almost-peak performers, the whole question of extrinsic versus intrinsic can become complicated. An extrinsic WIIFM can be converted into an intrinsic one *as soon as it is chosen independently by the performer.* Remember, for a worker to perform at her best, the locus of control must always lie within herself, not outside. This means that once a performer asks for an obviously extrinsic WIIFM (such as a manager's "order" to do a certain task) it is immediately and automatically converted into an intrinsic WIIFM.

> Jeff, a self-responsible performer, asked his manager if she wouldn't mind "ordering" him each day before leaving work to carefully clean up his workstation. Jeff explained that he loved working on his special projects but because he so often got caught up with the creative aspects of the work, he neglected to tidy up his workstation. And he knew that the next morning he would do a better job if he were able to work in an orderly environment instead of a pigsty. His manager, recognizing this as a WIIFM and a service to Jeff, was quick to oblige.

Even something as external as a pay increase becomes intrinsic if the performer requests it. For a self-responsible performer who says, "Since I am doing so well, I'd very much appreciate your giving me a larger share of the profits," simply because she requests it, making money becomes an intrinsic reward instead of an extrinsic one. By contrast, when a substandard or standard performer becomes motivated by a manager who says, "There's a larger share of the profits in store for you if you perform better," that's extrinsic motivation and doesn't lead to peak performance. A manager who has to dangle money in front of a performer as bait to motivate him can never expect a peak performance as the outcome.

WIIFMs for Probable Peak Performers

A self-responsible performer can find a sufficient reason to excel if one or two WIIFMs strike the proper sensitive nerve. The motivations listed below are some tried-and-true ways of rewarding self-responsible performers in business to encourage them to perform at peak.

WIIFM 1: Trusting and Being Trusted. For some, trusting and being trusted is a critical value.

> Will, age 38, is project director for a Canadian food products distributing company. He delegated the responsibility for heading up one of his most difficult projects to Paula, a twenty-four-year-old, self-responsible performer. Will was delighted to find that this young woman not only filled his shoes expertly but that she even managed to restart the quality control monitors that had long been out of operation. He was more than a little astonished at her proficiency and accomplishments. In this case, offering the WIIFM of trusting had a high payoff.

Self-responsible, effective-thinking performers find it easier than most to trust and be trusted because they often see it in their own best interests to be loyal. They are realists, and they know that if they are loyal to the company in rough times, this will eventually pay off.

WIIFM 2: A Mutual Mission. As a matter of principle, one of the best overall WIIFMs for motivating your self-responsible workers is to see to it that they each receive a fair share of the action. This does not necessarily mean an equal share of the profits. A fair share of the action means a share of the excitement and the payoffs (and the losses), a share in the responsibility for leadership, a share in establishing the corporate (or departmental) vision, mission, and goals, and a share of the authority and responsibility for making the operation a success.

Participation in establishing (or revising) the company mission or certain other goals can help motivate a self-responsible performer. If you get your peak performers involved at the ground floor in setting organizational or departmental goals, these workers have a psychological "buy-in." They believe that the department's or company's mission is their mission as well.

A sample of the kind of communication that can prove helpful in involving people in developing a company or departmental mission statement is shown in Figure 11-1.

In any case, do involve your people in setting goals so that they feel as if they are partners rather than merely pawns.

One word of caution: If you do not follow up or use any of the ideas you are offered, you may find mutual mission work demotivating instead of motivating.

WIIFM 3: TQM. The management philosophy known as total quality management (TQM) and most of the other quality-focused programs with acronyms, such as ISO-9000, SPC, DOE, and QFD, are useful incentives for peak performance if administered properly. They each have structured within them a variety of provisions that require peak performers, from the top of the company to the bottom, to be very much involved in the process of producing a high-quality product.

However, one important piece that is missing from each of these quality-oriented programs is a plan for developing total quality people—TQP.

WIIFM 4: Benchmarking. Another process that rewards peak performers is known as benchmarking. It actively involves people in establishing their own high standards for job performance.

Benchmarking in essence is a method of comparing the quality of a particular company's production with the actual production standards that are pervasive in a given industry. This process can promote a greater quality awareness among performers at all levels.

WIIFM 5: Quality Circles. The quality circle concept that is used so successfully in Japan can also work equally well in creating peak performer motivation. Ideally, in a sound quality cir-

Figure 11-1. Sample communication: Asking for input.

Dear _____:

As you may know, periodically we attempt to clarify the primary mission of our [company/department]. And this time, we very definitely need your help *before* we put the new mission statement into print.

Therefore, would you kindly list below your thoughts about what might be the best possible mission for the [company/department]? In a couple of weeks I'll be meeting with you and at that time I should like to discuss your ideas in detail. Please know that if you'd like to discuss any of your ideas with me before our scheduled meeting, I will be glad to meet with and learn from you even sooner.

Some of my ideas for the "best mission for our [company/department]" today are as follows:

_____

_____

_____

_____

_____

_____

_____

_____

_____

_____ (Use other side of form if necessary.)

cle program, performers at all levels regularly brainstorm ways of improving the quality of the products and/or services of the company.

The biggest problem with the use of quality circles in the United States is that there has not always been a sufficient commitment to the concept. An organization must take the quality recommendations made by its performers seriously—if the quality circle concept is to work.

WIIFM 6: A Mutual, Measurable Objective. Another program, the classic management by objectives (MBO) method of management guru Peter Drucker, is still another sound way for actively involving peak performers in the setting of goals. To create a proper MBO program, management and the performers must first agree on the value of a particular objective before anyone tries to measure that objective. Mismanagement of the MBO method has prevented it from realizing its full potential in building a peak performance organization.

Lee Iacocca used the MBO method most successfully in salvaging Chrysler. Iacocca enjoyed, he said recently, sitting down with his top managers and together establishing a few measurable objectives; then he periodically checked to see how they were doing and asked them from time to time if they needed any help. If they were doing fine, he stayed out of their way. If they needed help, he gave it to them. And if their objectives needed revision because they were too unrealistic, he helped them modify their goals to something more in keeping with the pragmatics of the situation. And it was this uncomplicated system (agreeing upon mutual objectives) that led to his much-publicized history of peak performance successes.

Tied in with the concept of achieving an objective is the concept of merit pay. While merit pay programs are complex to administer, when properly administered they can prove very effective. The difficulty with merit pay is that such a pay scale is often subjectively determined and in the process becomes a political football.

WIIFM 7: Quality Work Life. Another successful procedure for having self-responsible performers buy in to the mission of the company is called the Quality of Work Life (QWL) program. In this kind of program, everything possible is done to make sure that the work is meaningful for the performers. This is accomplished by allowing flexible work schedules, increasing the variety of work done by individuals, allowing workers to complete whole tasks rather than just parts of tasks, and so on. This arrangement works well but can fail if there is insufficient commitment on the part of management to train its performers in the value of such a program.

WIIFM 8: More Money. Money is the most common reward, but its usefulness is often misunderstood. The receipt of money is external. The reason that individuals want money varies: to buy necessities such as food, shelter, and clothing, as well as to impress others, to buy material gifts for oneself and others, or to give to charity. With money one can certainly buy material possessions, and with lots of money one can also buy prestige and influence in certain quarters.

All performances "appropriately reinforced" by money will tend to be repeated. But, as a motivational device, money has many shortcomings. Frederick I. Herzberg, a motivational authority in the 1950s, found that while a worker can at first be motivated by money, once that worker has received what he perceives to be fair pay, compared with what like workers elsewhere get, then money as a motivator loses most of its power.

Interestingly, money as a reinforcer quickly reaches a point of diminishing returns. In fact, as motivators go, money tends to be one of the least cost-effective. For example, research has shown that only very large amounts of money will induce someone to move after a certain level of income has been attained. At that break point, small amounts of money have very little effect; yet paying the money, even small amounts, is costly for the company. It is at this point that other motivators become much more effective. On most jobs, if the person doing the motivating is imaginative, many things can be found that are infinitely more effective as motivators than money alone.

WIIFM 9: Psychic Income. Psychic income is the term for all sorts of intangible rewards that people find valuable—the very kind of rewards that are likely to appeal to self-responsible peak performers. Psychic income includes such motivators as:

▲ Prestige
▲ Power
▲ Interesting work
▲ Opportunities for winning

▲ Feeling important
▲ Opportunities to learn new skills
▲ Recognition
▲ Warmer relationships with people
▲ Opportunities to realize hopes and dreams
▲ A feeling of usefulness

Of course, people can't eat psychic income, so real income should come first. But psychic income has much value too, especially for self-motivated people.

The WIIFM Principle in Review

Remember, at bottom, all persons are motivated by self-interest, the "What's in it for me?" principle. Standard and substandard workers are responsive to external motivations. But because it is your objective to develop self-responsible, self-motivated peak performers, using internal WIIFMs becomes more important. Self-motivated peak performers do not require pushing. Instead, they tend to push themselves toward higher and higher levels of performance. And they have a tendency to resist, and even to revolt, when someone pushes something on them.

All the traditional motivational devices (money, rewards, prestige, recognition) are essentially extrinsic. However, all motivational devices and tactics become intrinsic when they are provided solely on the request of the performer. Use the WIIFM principle to motivate all your workers to perform at peak, and then once you have such workers, do your best to keep them that way.

A Success Story in the Making

To help us fully understand the three-step system for creating peak performance, let's look in on a real-life situation. Meet Harry.

Harry was transferred into Mary's department some six months ago. Mary had no choice in the matter, but simply had to accept Harry Workman "as is." He was assigned, as is so often the case, by the powers that be.

Mary is a peak performance manager. She considers all her direct reports as "possible" peak performers, even if they are not yet fully self-responsible. Unfortunately, Harry has had a poor track record. Mary noticed right away that Harry Workman had consistently failed to take responsibility for his own performances. He often blamed other people for his job shortcomings and rarely took charge of his own performances.

Mary quickly enrolled Harry in her regular lunch-hour self-responsibility seminar. The topic: effective thinking and taking charge of the world from the neck up. And Harry turned out to be an excellent learner. In relatively short order, Harry stopped looking for someone or something to take the blame for his inadequate job performances, and instead took charge of his own actions. After Harry completed the self-responsibility training program—tops in the class—Mary upgraded him from a possible to a probable peak performer.

Mary then moved on to Step 2 of the system and made available to Harry a wide range of sufficient reasons (WIIFMs) for him to *want* to perform at peak. But she still does not know exactly which WIIFMs have just the right appeal to move Harry to his full measure of peak performance. That's where mentoring, counseling, and coaching know-how come into play. And these are the subject of Part IV.

Part IV

Nurturing Peak Performance

A company will get peak performances out of its work force only if it has either trained its people to be totally self-responsible or hired only those who already are. Once self-responsibility for performance and a sufficient reason to perform at peak are established, you will have performers who are ready to go on to their own high levels of peak performance. This is where Step 3 of the Creating PPM system comes into play.

At Step 3, you help nurture these team members into being practicing peak performers through a process of mentoring, counseling, and coaching. And then stay out of their way.

Once you have all your workers functioning at peak, you will have created a departmental or organizational peak performance zone where self-motivated peak performance becomes the norm.

Chapter 12
Mentoring

The best managers tend to see themselves as helpers of their people, as guides who help their direct reports to realize their highest individual performance levels. Although they are excellent leaders, they exert their greatest influence on their best people largely through mentoring them.

They predicate their mentoring on one basic assumption—that their mentoree is taking total self-responsibility for her own performances. They never, ever impose their mentoring on one of their qualified workers. They believe that if they did so, such superimposition would only lessen that performer's self-responsibility tendencies—quite the opposite of the goal intended.

Let all your self-responsible peak performers know that you are willing to mentor them *if* they continue to be self-responsible and *if* they request your help. Point out that you will never impose your mentoring, counseling, and coaching on them, but that it is there for them to take advantage of if they so desire it.

Presumably, your probable peak performers now respect you for all the right reasons. For example, they believe that:

▲ You serve as an excellent model for them to emulate in many ways.
▲ You take full responsibility for all your own performances.
▲ You have identified WIIFMs that make you want to perform at peak.
▲ You are a self-motivated peak performer in your own right.

▲ You have some valuable insights and wisdom about the job, the world of work, and life that are worth learning about.

In point of fact, true peak performers will jump at the chance to be mentored by you.

What Is a Mentor?

The word *mentor* is derived from a character in Homer's *Odyssey*. It literally means "a wise and trustworthy sage and adviser." Mentor was the loyal adviser to his friend Odysseus. Because Odysseus so respected Mentor, he entrusted him with the full care and education of his young son, Telemachus.

When you mentor your peak performers, that means you take a special interest in them. You must be prepared to offer them assistance that may well go beyond the standard call of duty.

As a peak performance mentor, you will use whatever you need within the full range of motivational artillery to advance your mentorees to peak level. You'll pull out all the stops. But remember, first and foremost, whatever strategy you use must serve to reinforce self-motivated, consistent, and durable peak performance. And it is only the intrinsic motivations that will lead to the objective of *sustained peak performance*.

What Makes a Good Mentor?

You mentor best if you are:

▲ Something of an authority in your field
▲ Influential within the company
▲ Have a vested interest in the professional growth and development of your mentoree
▲ Willing to commit the necessary time and emotional energy required to make the mentoring worthwhile
▲ Secure enough not to be threatened by other people's success

What Can Mentoring Accomplish?

Mentoring offers many practical advantages:

- ▲ It provides your mentoree with an inside track and helps him to deal effectively with the often confusing politics of the workplace.
- ▲ It helps your mentoree to avoid traps that ensnare the unsophisticated.
- ▲ It helps your mentoree to move his career forward, to work his way upward, perhaps even to surpass you.
- ▲ It reinforces within your mentoree the twin objectives (self-responsibility and sufficient WIIFM) that lead to peak performance.

How Do You Go about Mentoring?

You can bolster your mentoree's self-esteem by sharing in his dreams. But mostly, as a mentor, you provide wise counsel, coaching advice, and support. In addition, you do your best to help your mentoree understand the secrets you've probably learned the hard way about the nuances of the corporate structure, its special politics, and its key players.

When you mentor someone, you offer special help—whatever it takes to guide that person through the rocks and shoals of corporate life. You might, for example, say things like this:

"Don't spend too much time on that project; the president has already hinted he's thinking of scrapping it."

"You can socialize with that person, but do it outside the company. He doesn't have as much influence as he would like you to think."

"Rewrite this. The vice president has a thing about that word. It's a pet peeve of hers."

"You should sign up for this workshop; the general manager notices when people take extra classes."

"The best thing you can do for your career is to get into this management training program. And yes, I'll write a good recommendation for you."

"If you ever get a chance to go on a sales trip with the president, do it! And brush up on your tennis; he plays hard and he respects people who give him a good game."

"I know you're not excited about more schooling, but you must know that you need that MBA to get ahead in this organization."

"I'm glad you asked me about that: It is hard to get work done when people interrupt you all the time. Here are a couple of tricks I've learned."

One of your most important responsibilities is to provide honest feedback to your mentoree on how you view her progress. Here are a few examples:

"You did a good job on the Lindsey project, but you'll need to look for ways to work faster. The boss understands it's your first time as project manager, but next time he'll expect to see fewer hours."

"Nobody I ever knew really *liked* making speeches, but it was pretty obvious you were nervous up there. Here's some information on a class you might want to think about."

"I saw how you handled that unhappy customer; that was terrific. You have a natural flair for working with people."

"I don't want to see you develop a reputation for being hard to work with. Nobody doubts your talent, but this firm really puts a lot of emphasis on teamwork. When they say they look for team players, they really mean it."

You should make yourself available to your mentoree, not for dealing with all his problems and frustrations, but available enough to help him over some of the rough spots.

In your work as a mentor, you will need to be expert in using both counseling and coaching skills. Those skills are described in the next two chapters. Mentoring includes counseling and coaching but goes beyond them. As a mentor, you take a very special interest in your mentoree because he has met your peak performer qualifications. As such, you might find that he needs your help in clarifying which of the various reasons available to him are sufficiently appealing to make him want to perform at peak level. This is one purpose of counseling—to clarify these reasons. Then, in conjunction with your counseling, you might very well find that you need to coach him as well.

Some Cautions about Mentoring

There may be an occasion or two when your mentoree will ask you to provide him with the impetus of a stern directive. At first glance, doing so might seem to be highly autocratic on your part. But it isn't really. For example, if your mentoree says, "Please order me to call on that very difficult account *because* I could use a little urging on your part," you may do so—but only because your mentoree *asks* for that directive. Any directive becomes automatically intrinsic if it is requested. In every case, it is essential that your mentoree continue to feel self-responsible and to pursue in his own way his own special reasons for wanting to excel. As mentor, you are to do everything possible to help your mentoree make maximum use of his own talents.

Another caution. Please be sure *not to serve* as a mentor to any one of your workers who fails to take total self-responsibility. These standard or below-standard performers can be considered peak performer trainees. But until they take self-responsibility, they will be depending upon you for leadership. Of course, you can counsel and coach them along the way, but reserve your role as mentor for the time when they deserve it, for when they begin to take full charge of themselves.

Your groomed peak performer must take an active role in all the mentoring you do. It will not be useful for you to do any commanding, because that would only serve to set a poor example for a peak performer and might weaken his resolve to attain peak level out of his own self-motivation.

But remember, you never impose your mentoring, counseling, or coaching on your mentoree, because one of your prime objectives is to keep your mentoring self-responsible. All the mentoring, counseling, and coaching you do must facilitate, not detract from, your mentoree being a self-responsible performer.

What's in It for You?

The rewards of mentoring good people can be enormous. Here are two examples of what successful mentors have to say:

> Ralph, age 46, is the news director and head of a large city newspaper: "I loved being a news hound. They say I was pretty good at it in my day. But sharing what I learned the hard way, and helping younger reporters to make the grade, that's an even greater pleasure."

> Jack, 49, is senior partner of a large law firm: "I can't tell you how proud I am that young Bradley has become a full partner. What I've learned to respect most about Brad is his fire, his ambition, and his love for the environment. I like that. He's a real competitor. Wants to be the very best. And he has wonderful values. He really cares about what is happening to our environment.
>
> "Seeing young Brad be promoted to full partner in less than six years was a great thrill for me. I brought Brad into this firm because I liked his values and his passion for a cause. And because I could see, even then, that he had great potential. I did all I could to help him along. Taught him the ropes, so to speak. And in a few years I expect him to surpass me, be better than I am on this job. Believe me, nothing would give me greater pleasure."

Chapter 13
Counseling

Counseling is a part of mentoring, but it is not the same thing. You will remember that mentoring—which involves taking a special interest in someone and giving that person special help—is something you reserve for those who have already demonstrated that they are able to take self-responsibility, and only for those who ask for it.

Counseling, on the other hand, is useful for everyone. In fact, I recommend that you schedule some kind of open-ended counseling session with all your staff members on a regular basis.

Let's first make a distinction between *counseling* and *coaching*. In counseling, your job is to get to know the person you are counseling. You're concentrating on the whole person. Your job is to help your counselee to *clarify* his own motivational directions, to balance his inner compass, and to begin to figure out who he really is and what he really wants out of his job and his life.

Coaching, by contrast, deals with specific problems and performance skills. It is solution-oriented. It is pragmatic and down-to-earth. It focuses on finding solutions or at least figuring out better ways to cope with specific personal and professional issues. Coaching requires its own special know-how, and is explained in Chapter 14.

However, there is an important link between the two. One of the main purposes of counseling is to enable you to know the person well enough that you can help pinpoint the specific WIIFMs that appeal to him, and to uncover areas where coaching is needed.

Client-Centered Counseling

Peak performance counseling relies on a very specific approach known as client-centered counseling. It was originated in the 1940s by Dr. Carl Rogers. Client-centered counseling is *not* psychoanalysis, which concentrates to a great extent on reviewing the past, especially problems originating in childhood. It is also *not* gestalt therapy, a kind of emotional treatment that often leads to revisiting past emotional upsets and working them through in the present. And it is *not* behavioral counseling, which pays much more attention to the environment influencing human behavior than it does to the individual's responsibility for shaping it.

Dr. Rogers's client-centered model of counseling is, without question, the counseling method of choice to help probable peak performers remain self-responsible as they move upward into actual peak performance. Client-centered peak performance counseling is the kind of counseling that helps the counselee take full self-responsibility and clarify his reasons (if any) for genuinely wanting to perform at peak in a given instance.

To do client-centered counseling, all you need is to possess three key qualities: (1) effective thinking know-how; (2) a capacity to care about your counselee's feelings (empathy); and (3) the ability to refrain from giving advice.

What About Special Training?

Counseling is part of the role of all good managers. Some believe that counseling should be done only by professional psychotherapists. But, in reality, counseling is much too important to be left exclusively to the so-called professionals. Peak performance managers can train themselves to become well-qualified client-centered counselors to all of their people, and especially to their probable peak performers.

The main qualification is that you genuinely care about the counselee. And caring is a product of thought choice. After all, the peak performance manager is an expert in effective thought choosing. By applying thought choice, you can readily do all the things that are required to be an excellent client-centered counselor:

- ▲ You can choose to care.
- ▲ You can choose to be empathetic and understanding.
- ▲ You can willfully become a sounding board for your performer.
- ▲ You can decide in advance of the session that you are going to listen to feelings.

However, common sense should tell you that there are limits to what you can do. If you sense that your counselee is seriously troubled about something, or facing personal or family difficulties that are beyond your sphere of influence, the compassionate thing to do is to suggest professional help. Facilitate this process as much as you can; help the counselee make the right connections through your company's employee assistance program, if there is one. But realize your limits.

The Purpose of Counseling

Client-centered peak performance counseling is, at bottom, a conversation between two people. It differs from an ordinary conversation, however, in that it is essentially one-sided. It focuses entirely on the life, needs, desires, and concerns of the counselee and not the counselor. It is designed to have the counselee ultimately help himself by becoming more self-responsible. And with inner-directed, self-motivated types of people it is received on a voluntary basis.

In this kind of counseling, at least 80 percent of the talking is done by the counselee, who will talk almost entirely about himself—his own feelings and concerns, not other people's, and most certainly not about the counselor's feelings and concerns.

Sometimes very self-reliant people consider it a sign of weakness to ask for counseling help. But the truth of the matter is that even the best of us, from time to time, can find the pressures of business and personal life, the pressures of decision making, and sometimes just the pressures of day-to-day coping a bit overwhelming. And when that happens, it is extremely useful to obtain some help in getting over these hurdles.

Client-centered counseling can help a counselee to deal more effectively with such subjective and personal questions as, "Where am I going with my life?" "My career?" "This company?" "This kind of work?" And counseling often raises even deeper questions. "Who are you, really?" "What is it that you really want." "What's the best and worst of life as you have experienced it thus far?" "What are your basic values?" Client-centered counseling helps the counselee probe beneath his own surface.

There are several areas where client-centered counseling can definitely be of enormous help. It can, for instance, help the counselee to:

▲ Continue to take full responsibility
▲ Clarify career directions
▲ Improve job satisfaction
▲ Adjust to innovations and changes on the job
▲ Gain greater self-confidence
▲ Deal more effectively with stress

And it can help the counselor to know the counselee much better so that together they may locate a WIIFM or two powerful enough to move the counselee to want to perform at peak.

Conducting a Counseling Session

Conducting a client-centered counseling session, especially the first session with a particular counselee, involves five steps:

1. In advance of the initial session, complete a pre-counseling empathy form (see below) regarding the counselee.

2. When the counselee enters your office, be sure to establish a sufficient degree of comfort and rapport between you, as counselor and counselee, that the sessions will be productive.

Assure the counselee that what you are about to discuss is completely confidential. Set a specific time frame (usually no more than forty minutes) for the session. Then open the counseling session. Some possible "openers" will be discussed later in this chapter.

3. Help your counselee to identify an area of focus for the session. Keep the focus open-ended—until the counselee defines and clarifies the agenda. If an area of focus does not emerge after a while, you may suggest that you would like to concentrate on the personal and professional life history of the counselee.

4. Listen deeply and empathetically, but refrain from giving any advice. Don't forget that one of your main duties is to develop or sustain a self-responsible performer. Within this context, you should remain as nonjudgmental as possible.

5. Move to closing the session within the time allotted. Be sure to suggest a voluntary follow-up session if one seems appropriate and if the counselee shows signs of wanting to take advantage of such an offer. Always give your counselee some kind of "psychological homework" to do after the session.

Developing Empathy

Probably the most important element in successful counseling is taking a posture of active caring. That's where empathy comes in. Empathy means that you put yourself in the other person's shoes. When you do that, it's impossible *not* to care about that person's problems and concerns.

In order to get you thinking in advance about your counselee, it is advisable for you to complete a precounseling empathy form like the one below. This activity can help you to be sufficiently empathetic during the course of the counseling session. It can also give you some ideas regarding a possible agenda for the session should the counselee be hesitant or unclear about the point of the session. The items in the inventory can serve as areas you might want to have your counselee think and talk about.

A Pre-Counseling Empathy Form

On the following worksheet, please complete all of the unfinished sentences about a specific performer, one whom you expect to counsel. While pretending you are that performer, try to enter his perceptual world, seeing things just as he sees them. In completing the sentences below, if you currently have insufficient information, make a guess just the same. Your first impulse, aided by imagination, can often be on target.

Date:_____

Counselee's name:_____

Job title:_____

Duties:_____

_____

_____

Instructions: Complete the following sentences as if you were the counselee. Try to enter the perceptual world of your counselee. Use your best guess to complete each sentence. Your intuition may, in fact, be your best guide.

1. Regarding my job, I feel

_____

_____

_____

2. Regarding my boss [*actually you*], I secretly feel that he or she should

_____

_____

_____

3. Regarding the taking care of fine details on my job, I feel that

_____

_____

_____

4. My main goal in life is to

_____

_____

_____

5. If it weren't so embarrassing, I'd tell you the following about me

_____

_____

_____

6. My most serious personal weakness is

_____

_____

_____

7. My greatest professional strength is

_____

_____

_____

8. Regarding the making of more money, I feel

_____

_____

_____

9. At work, what gives me the greatest pleasure is

_____

_____

_____

10. I appreciate it when my boss [*that's really you*]

_____

_____

_____

11. Regarding job advancement, I want

_____

_____

_____

12. I need recognition for

_____

_____

_____

13. I resent my boss [*you, again*] when

_____

_____

_____

14. I feel that my colleagues

_____

_____

_____

15. I could do a little bit better on this job if only

_____

_____

_____

16. My boss [*that's you again*] could get so much more out of me if only

_____

_____

_____

Once you have done your best to complete the form, you will be in a good position to conduct a "getting to know you better" counseling session. During this session, concentrate on genuinely appreciating and understanding your performer and try to see if your guesses about him were on target.

Opening the Initial Session

The first thing to do in your initial session is to concentrate on establishing a sufficient level of rapport. Get comfortable with each other. Establishing rapport often involves a bit of small talk. "Jim, good to see you. How are things going?" Or "Jim, it was great seeing you at the company meeting. You sure had some good ideas." In order for the performer to feel comfortable in the role of counselee, it is first necessary for the manager to be comfortable in his role as counselor.

In some instances, the initial session will focus entirely on the counselee's personal life history. But many people don't find it easy to talk about themselves, and so the counselee may be more comfortable talking strictly about work issues.

In either case, your job is to listen without making any judgmental statements. Really concentrate on the feelings of the counselee as he begins to share. You may find, as the session progresses, that you have verified your speculations. Or you might find that you will have to modify or add to what you know about the counselee. Your goal in the counseling process is to understand him better and to find out what it is that makes him tick.

Listening to Feelings

If your counselee has a difficult time doing most of the talking, you may have to ask some probing questions. Other counselees are like a dam of water that has suddenly given way; they just talk and talk. But don't encourage too much idle chatter. Your job is to have the counselee talk about his feelings and about things and events that were important in his life.

Once the counselee gets talking, make every attempt to listen empathically. Concentrate less on the content of what the counselee is saying and more on the tone of what is being said. The counselee will do about 80 percent of the talking. Listen primarily to the feelings of your counselee. Use the word *feel* often during the session. For example:

Counselee: It was very difficult to set out on my own after I finished school. I wasn't used to being on my own very much.

Counselor: How did you *feel* being on your own?

Counselee: I didn't like it. It was scary.

When the counselee talks about his feelings, it is important to empathize with him and refrain from giving advice. Empathy means that you put yourself, temporarily, in the shoes of the performer. For example:

Counselor [*reflecting empathy*]: I see. You were a bit frightened. It wasn't easy for you. Right?

Counselee: Right. You got it.

Try to be totally nonjudgmental. It would be judgmental to say, for example, "Jim, you shouldn't let being on your own get to you." Just make comments that let the counselee know you truly understand what he is saying.

Showing You Care

During the counseling session, convey your caring by reflecting an appreciation of all your counselee's feelings. Enter into your counselee's emotional world if he allows you to. Above all, avoid giving advice or making a judgment on any aspect of your counselee's life. Just appreciate and try to understand.

To show that you appreciate the counselee's feelings, say so directly or indirectly by your own sounds ("ummhuh"), your own body language (moving your head understandingly, nodding, making appropriate eye contact), and the words you use to paraphrase or reflect what the counselee has said.

If you don't understand, don't pretend that you do. Stop him from speaking and ask for further clarification or for examples. Be especially attuned to nonverbal communication signals. Look at the performer's body language. His eyes. Facial expressions. Read the feeling tone that so often expresses itself in intangible ways.

Don't worry about pauses or long silences. Don't rush. In fact, slow down. And have the performer slow down as well. Don't interrupt him, and don't permit outside interruptions during the counseling session. Twenty high-quality minutes of deep and honest listening to feelings are worth much more than twenty hours of superficial listening.

Good and Bad Responses

There are five categories of response to an individual's statements. In the context of counseling, some are good and some are bad.

1. The *evaluation response* is typically a judgmental statement indicating some standard that is acceptable. "You shouldn't do that. You should do something more useful." This is not an appropriate response when doing client-centered counseling.

2. The *interpretive response* is typically a statement that makes a conjecture as to the personality dynamics of the individual. "You probably did that because you are insecure." This, also, is not an appropriate response when doing client-centered counseling.

3. The *probing response* is an attempt to gain more information. "Why did you do that?" This can be useful if used appropriately and sparingly. It is usually more useful to permit the counselee to develop his own flow and rhythm during the ses-

sion. But if the counselee seems stuck too often, probing may help him unwind.

4. The *supportive response* is an attempt to encourage the taking of immediate steps to ameliorate the individual's difficulty. "Go for it. Take these tests and be on time tomorrow and you'll be on track." This is a value judgment and should be avoided.

5. The *understanding response* is one that typically reflects back the content and some of the feeling tone of the individual's statement. "I can appreciate that. You work hard and you feel pressure from doing that." This is one of the most useful kinds of responses in client-centered counseling. Understanding should reflect simple empathy rather than unalloyed sympathy.

Encouraging the Sharing of Information

As your counselees become more comfortable talking about themselves, they will gradually share more information. Make good use of every opportunity to learn more about them.

For instance, let's eavesdrop on a session. Through gentle questions, the counselor, Elizabeth, has encouraged Jim, the counselee, to honestly share his feelings about his work, and Jim has admitted, a little sheepishly, that some of the enjoyment has gone out of his job.

Elizabeth: Can you find anything about your job that will make you feel that what you are doing is really important?

Jim: I'll have to think about that. You've certainly gone all out to have me enjoy the work. It's just that I don't feel as if it is taking me where I want to go.

Elizabeth: What are you aiming for? Where would you like to be at this point in your career, at your age? Is there anything you can think of that could help you to enjoy your work more?

Notice that Elizabeth did not become defensive or attempt to superimpose her values on Jim. She did not say, for example,

"Jim, you ought to enjoy your work. You're well paid. Plenty of people would be thrilled to have your job." She simply tried to understand, to appreciate, and to reflect. Her purpose was to have Jim understand himself better.

Later on in the session (or during a later session), Elizabeth will ask Jim what he proposes to do about his low job satisfaction. She will not take on the responsibility for fixing the problem. But she will help Jim to take ownership of his own issue. And she will help Jim to figure out his own way either of solving the problem or of coping with it more effectively.

To be sure, she will remind Jim at some point that he is a thought chooser. And that the power to choose effective thoughts that will help him to find a greater satisfaction in his work lies within him.

Ending the Session

Finally, be sure to move the counseling session to a close within the time allotted. Sometimes the counselee wants to go on and on. In such cases, stand up. The counselee will follow your lead. Suggest, if it makes sense, another session. But this time put the responsibility for moving toward it in the hands of the performer. Explain that all counseling sessions after the first session will be by counselee request. Of course, be sure to express your availability.

Counseling sessions often progress into coaching sessions. At this point, the manager, who has been serving as counselor and perhaps as mentor, takes on an additional role: that of coach.

Chapter 14
Coaching

Peak performance managers, as part of their mentoring function, serve as expert coaches to their qualified probable peak performers. Their coaching is *peak performance-focused*. As coaches, peak performance managers provide the kind of wisdom that enables the coachee to reduce the given problem to a manageable size, both externally and internally.

Peak performance coaching focuses on the specifics of the worker's performance. Through coaching, you help good performers become even better by showing them how to make specific, concrete improvements in their work.

Coaching makes direct use of this well-known saying: "Give me the courage to change those things that I can change, the strength to accept those things over which I have little or no control, and the wisdom to know the difference." Here's how one manager puts this dictum into practice.

> "I help my people turn whatever problem they are facing into a manageable project," says Saul, age 65, the president of a bedding manufacturing company. "In order to do that, I've got to get a clear understanding of the issue. And then, together, we come up with a plan for dealing with it."

When to Use Coaching

Coaching can be used in many different kinds of circumstances. It can, for instance, help in:

▲ Zeroing in on a "sufficient WIIFM" to enable the coachee to perform at peak level

▲ Improving job performance
▲ Conducting a performance review
▲ Following up on a performance review
▲ Improving a job-related skill (such as an interpersonal skill, a communication skill, a machinery operation skill)
▲ Giving the coachee a better understanding of the nuances of corporate culture and politics
▲ Dealing more effectively with a difficult colleague, boss, or direct report
▲ Improving a minor aspect of the coachee's personality (such as becoming more assertive, more cooperative, more tactful, less worried, less procrastinating, less perfectionist)

Making a Two-Pronged Attack

Show your coachees how to attack difficulties by taking a two-pronged approach. This means showing them how to tackle a problem from two directions simultaneously—from both the inside and the outside.

Explain to them how they can attack the disturbing issue *attitudinally* through thinking effective thoughts and, at the same time, *practically* by taking concrete actions and steps. More specifically, while they apply "the self-responsibility sentence" to choose those thoughts that will place them in an optimal frame of mind, they concurrently take whatever practical measures are necessary to ease or eliminate the upsetting situation.

Explain to your coachees that when nothing else remains, they can still change the thoughts that they are choosing. Explain to them how they can pause and replace any defective thoughts that they may be choosing with effective ones.

In other words, have your coachee make full use of the self-responsibility imperative: "Whenever necessary, pause and think and then choose effective thoughts!"

Peak Performance Coaching in Action

Budding peak performer Malcolm, a salesman, has been trained to take self-responsibility and has found "sufficient WIIFM" to want to be the best salesman in the company. But he still needs more know-how. He asks for some good mentoring, and he gets it. Verna, his manager, mentor, counselor, and now coach, comes to his assistance. Let's watch how it works.

> *Coaching issue:* How Malcolm can close a greater percentage of his sales
> *Scene:* Verna's office
> *Objective:* Reinforcing self-responsibility and validating his "sufficient WIIFM," plus the immediate objective of coaching Malcolm on sound techniques for becoming "a better closer"

The coaching aspect of mentoring does not deal with Malcolm's personality in the way that it would if it were a counseling session. Instead, it focuses on his behavior, in this case his need for a higher ratio of closings to calls. Verna makes sure that in everything she says she separates Malcolm's selling performance from other dimensions of his personality.

Coach: Malcolm, you say that your sales closing performance is not up to your own standard. I agree. Your percentage of closings is not up to snuff.

Coach Verna makes sure that she does not criticize coachee Malcolm's personality, only his performance. In fact, she lets him point out his own shortcoming. Having a coachee remain dignified is very important. Coaching is really wise advising. The coach gives clear and specific advice to improve the coachee's performance.

Coach: Malcolm, try assuming the sale. And asking for a deposit instead of just hoping for a close. Ask your customer to buy. Don't be afraid. If you do this, Malcolm, I think you'll find your percentage of closings improving.

That's very specific, constructive advice about performance.

In your coaching session, take a few minutes to establish rapport as quickly as possible and then try to get directly to the point. It is not helpful to anyone, particularly the coachee, if you

Figure 14-1. The six steps of formal coaching.

1. Help the coachee to identify and clarify the nature of the specific issue.
2. Help the coachee to identify those externals (if any) that can be changed.
3. Help the coachee to identify (a) a particular aspect of his or her own behavior that can be changed; and (b) the effective thoughts that will lead to that behavior change.
4. Help the coachee to develop and decide upon a plan of action.
5. Help the coachee to move into action.
6. Follow up and evaluate the effectiveness of the action taken.

evade the central issue, even if it is embarrassing to deal with it. Stalling or beating about the bush will serve only to increase the anxiety level of the employee whom you have called to your office instead of reducing it. Here's what you can say:

Coach: Jerry, your market strategy forecast reports have been coming in too late, much after our deadline, and they are not doing us much good if they come in that late. I want to talk to you about that.

Coach: Ed, I called you in to discuss the personality conflict you are having with the director of purchasing. I want to help you to resolve it. It's getting in the way of our operations, and we've got to bring it to a head.

Once the issue is on the table, the two of you can quickly come to a clearer understanding of its nature. Then, together, you can also figure out what can be done to change it, develop a plan of action, and determine a time frame for the action to take place. After the action has been taken, arrange for a follow-up and evaluation. All of this amounts to a six-step coaching procedure, outlined in Figure 14-1.

The Six Steps in Detail

1. *Describe the specific issue.* After rapport has been established, have your performer clearly identify his or her problem.

It is best to have the worker state the issue in the form of a question. For example, "How can I deal more effectively with the purchasing agent?" or "What, specifically, can I do to earn a better, more favorable performance review next time?" The focus should be on the performance or behavior rather than the personality of the coachee.

2. *Identify and evaluate externals.* Identify the externals that can be changed. Ask your coachee to identify those things about other persons, places, or things central to this issue that she can change. Help her to figure out (by brainstorming) as many things that can be done to ameliorate the situation as possible. After this has been done, evaluate the practicality of each of these possibilities.

3a. *Identify and evaluate any problem behaviors.* Help the coachee to identify and list those aspects of his own behavior that can be changed in order to deal with the issue in question. Ask the coachee, "If it were somehow possible to change any aspect of your own behavior, what aspect of it would you like to change?" Have your coachee figure out the one or two aspects of his behavior he might change and then determine which one he would like to work on.

3b. *Identify and evaluate effective thoughts for dealing with external and internal actions.* Have your coachee identify effective thoughts that might prove helpful in dealing with the issue. (At this point, you might find it useful to skip ahead to Chapter 16 in order to preview some of the many possible effective thoughts.) What thoughts will help to change the externals previously identified? What thoughts will help in changing the coachee's own behavior? There are effective thoughts for changing any of one's own attitudes, feelings, or behaviors—if need be. Remind your coachee that, if nothing else, she can always choose any thought she wants to at any time and in any place.

4. *Develop an action plan.* Help your coachee develop a plan to deal with the situation. As part of the plan, develop both a best-case and a worst-case scenario. Have the coachee describe in detail how he now plans to attack the issue in question.

5. *Move the coachee into action.* Have your coachee commit himself to a specific time frame and schedule for implementing

his plan of action. Set a time for conducting a follow-up coaching session, the purpose of which is to determine the effectiveness of the chosen action plan.

6. *Follow up and evaluate the plan effected.* Set a specific time to get together again to review the results. If the plan worked—great! But if it didn't, help your coachee to develop and put into play a more effective action.

Realistically, not all problems are completely solvable. In fact, there are usually some elements of almost every problem that cannot be changed, no matter how cleverly or hard one works to change them. In these instances, remember the A-B-C method from Chapter 3. Make sure that you have tried thought-choosing plans A (Aggravation) and B (Branding). If you tried plans A and B and both proved insufficient, all that is left is Plan C (Closure).

The Coaching Worksheet

The coaching process has been condensed into a six-step coaching worksheet. You can use it to guide your coaching sessions, and then later your coachees can use it independently to review their progress. This kind of self-coaching will help your coachee become more self-responsible.

THE COACHING WORKSHEET

1. Describe your issue of concern, briefly, in the space below.

_____

_____

_____

2. Identify those external things that you can probably change.

_____

_____

_____

3. Identify: (a) an aspect of your own behavior that you can change if you put your mind to it.

_____

_____

_____

(b) the specific effective thoughts that may assist you (if you choose them) in changing the aspect of your behavior that you have identified. (Refer to the Starter File of Effective Thoughts in Chapter 16.)

_____

_____

_____

4. Develop an action plan. In outline form, write down the elements of it below.

_____

_____

_____

5. Move into action. List specific time frames for implementing the various parts of your action plan.

_____

_____

_____

6. Follow up on the results of your action plan, assessing them in the summary you write.

_____

_____

_____

    If your action plan didn't work, make a new one and try again. Write down what you'll do differently.

_____

_____

_____

    Remember, the one thing your coachees can always change is themselves. And all they need in order to do that is to choose thoughts that lead to that change.

Chapter 15
Self-Coaching

In Chapter 14 you learned how to coach people in specific areas where their performance was falling short. You learned a six-step coaching process built around the philosophy of choosing effective thoughts to modify behavior. And you learned that, ultimately, self-responsible people can do their own coaching, using the six-step coaching worksheet.

In this chapter we look more in depth at self-coaching. This is where the concepts of thought choosing and of self-responsibility come together. This is where you and your performers can see immediate changes.

In training your coachees to take charge of their own problems, have them practice by identifying an effective thought or two for each of the following exercises. Start by reviewing the list of twenty-four thought areas in Figure 15-1; you will probably also find it helpful to preview the full discussion of these same areas in Chapter 16.

Figure 15-1. Twenty-four areas for effective thoughts.

1. Aloneness	9. Guilt	17. Rejection
2. Approval	10. Help	18. Relationships
3. Body	11. Illness	19. Responsibility
4. Centering	12. Justice	20. Risking
5. Death	13. Lovability	21. Roles
6. Experience	14. Loving	22. Uniqueness
7. Facts	15. Now	23. Wholism
8. Feelings	16. Purpose	24. Worry

SELF-COACHING PRACTICE EXERCISES

1. Imagine that you work as a receptionist. You find a large rip in the seat of your dress just as you are about to report to work in the front office. What are some effective thoughts that might help you deal more effectively with this situation?

    _____

    _____

    _____

    _____

2. You are a salesperson. A business prospect has kept you waiting more than an hour for your appointment with him. What effective thoughts can help you here?

    _____

    _____

    _____

    _____

3. You are an up-and-coming manager. Yet the presentation you just gave to the board of directors is rated as "awful" by the persons who heard it. Write down the effective thoughts that you think can help you in these circumstances.

    _____

    _____

    _____

    _____

4. While you are waiting in a long line at the bank, the clerks seem to take an extended break. This is sure to make you late for your next appointment. List an effective thought or two for this situation.

_____

_____

_____

_____

5. You are in business for yourself, and business is very bad. You are becoming quite frightened over the possibility that you might go broke and get even deeper into debt. What thoughts might help you in this circumstance?

_____

_____

_____

_____

6. Your house was robbed and many of your most treasured possessions were taken. Are there any thoughts that might help you here?

_____

_____

_____

_____

7. You are the manager of the shipping department. One of your colleagues speaks at a business meeting and erroneously reports that it was your fault that the merchandise was not shipped on time. As a result of this failure, the company loses one of its key accounts. What are the effective thoughts that you might choose in this circumstance?

_____

_____

_____

_____

8. Your boss decides to pile more work on top of your already overburdened work load. What thoughts can reduce your anger and resentment over this event?

_____

_____

_____

_____

9. The production line breaks down. You are blamed even though it was in no way your responsibility. Are there any thoughts that could help you deal with this effectively?

_____

_____

_____

_____

10. An undeserving colleague of yours gets the promotion that you had expected. Which of the thought-choosing approaches— A, B, or C—will be most helpful here?

_____

_____

_____

_____

Self-Coaching in Action

Here are three common situations that might easily have arisen in your department. Each of the three people involved filled out a six-step coaching worksheet. If you were to mentor and coach the people facing these problems, how would you advise them to think through their situations?

Self-Coaching Case 1: Jonathan's Dilemma

Jonathan has a difficult person with whom he must deal on a regular basis. His coworker, Mark, has been with the company for several years longer than Jonathan has. Mark is very jealous of Jonathan's rapid success. And because of this he is uncooperative and does all he can to undermine Jonathan. Jonathan is very troubled over this. He has asked his manager to intervene, but his manager is not able to help. Figure 15-2 shows how Jonathan accomplished some very effective self-coaching.

Jonathan's line of effective thinking went something like this:

> "Mark doesn't really get on my nerves, it's my thoughts about Mark that get on my nerves. Consequently, all I need to do is to choose thoughts about Mark that don't get on my nerves. Better yet, I might choose to not even think about Mark. But first I'll meet with him and try to set him straight. After all, people (including Mark) tend to treat me the way that I teach them to treat me, at least over the long haul. I'll face off with him and let him know that I'm no pushover. I won't put this off. I know that this won't happen by osmosis. To me, facing off with Mark will be a risk, a kind of adventure. If it doesn't work, then I'll just have to go to plan B."

Self-Coaching Case 2: Marla's Presentation Fears

Marla has worked hard and is in line for a promotion. However, all her life she has had a tremendous fear of public speaking, and this is keeping her from advancing. She's determined to overcome her fear. Figure 15-3 illustrates Marla's self-coaching progress in dealing with the problem.

Figure 15-2. Jonathan's six-step self-coaching worksheet.

1. List your specific problem below.
   Mark, my coworker, is doing all that he can to sabotage my career. I do not enjoy working with him. Mark is obviously jealous of my success with the company.

2. Identify those externals that can be changed.
   a. I could go beyond my manager and seek intervention.
   b. I could leave this department, although, except for the trouble I'm having with Mark, I enjoy working here very much.
   c. I could meet with Mark and explain to him in no uncertain terms that his behavior is unacceptable.
   I believe that option c. has the most merit.

3a. Identify a particular aspect of your own behavior that can be changed.
   I could get tougher and stop letting Mark get away with sabotaging me.

   b. What are the effective thoughts that can help you to make that change?
   I believe that the following thoughts might prove effective for me in this instance: numbers 8, 13, 18, 20, and 24.

ET 8—Feelings: "Mark is not upsetting me, I'm upsetting me. I can choose thoughts that will help me to stop doing that to myself."

ET 13—Justice: "It may be unfair that Mark is trying to sabotage me, but I can handle the fact that life is unfair by working it through. Grieve for it, then work it positively from that point on."

ET 18—Rejection: "After all, no one can really reject me if they do not know me. It's just my image that is being rejected, not me."

ET 20—Responsibility: "It is I who am responsible for my own thoughts and for the feelings and behavior that result from those thoughts. Consequently, I can choose thoughts that not only keep Mark's jealous behavior from hindering me but allow me to do well in spite of Mark's sabotaging efforts."

ET 24—Worry: "It certainly pays to have due concern about this circumstance, but not worry. Worry is of no help, but effective thinking and effective actions are of great help."

4. Decide on a plan of action and write it down.
    Meet with Mark after work and set him straight.
    _____

5. Move into action. List a deadline for your planned action below.
    I've arranged to meet with him after work on November 4th.
    _____

6. Follow up and evaluate the effectiveness of the action taken.
    Incomplete at this point in time.
    _____

[Afterwards, Jonathan will assess the results of his action. If he is unsuccessful, he will start again at Step 1 and attempt to come up with some new ideas. If all this fails, he will resort to the A-B-Cs of thought choosing and make the best of the situation that way.]

Marla's basic line of effective thinking to help her overcome her fear of public speaking went something like this:

"Marla, you don't really fear public speaking. Rather, you are choosing thoughts about speaking that frighten you. Instead, Marla, choose some thoughts about speaking that will not frighten you. And don't delay in learning how to improve your presentational skills. After all, Marla, it's your professional life that's at stake. If you want to get ahead in your career and this fear of public speaking is getting in your way, conquer it. And don't count on someone else doing this for you. You can do it, and you've got to do it yourself. Don't worry about failing if your next speech isn't so well received. After all, Marla, you can't fail, because if, after your presentation, others don't like it, that will not be you they are rejecting but only your image, your performance. You are much more than your image. Remember, Marla, you don't have to give a great presentation. That's a preference, not a need. Keep that in mind. It will make doing it much easier. Remember, again, Marla, it is your current thoughts about giving presentations that have up-

Figure 15-3. Marla's six-step self-coaching worksheet.

1. List your specific problem below.
   I get extremely nervous when asked to make a public presentation or even when I have to stand up at a small meeting to say a few words. This is hampering my career. Last week I was invited to speak at the directors meeting. It could have meant great visibility for me. Instead, I got so worried that I called in sick to the office that morning. Someone else took my place. The truth is, I had become so nervous that I found an excuse not to show up.

2. Identify and evaluate those externals (if any) that can be changed.
   a. I could get a different kind of job. (Not acceptable to me.)
   b. I could settle for not being able to do this. (No, I'm not giving up.)
   c. I could continue to find excuses every time I am asked to speak. (This doesn't make sense any more. I've done that too many times already.)
   d. I could take a course in presentational skills. (Good idea.)
   e. I could try self-hypnosis. (I'll give it a shot. Why not?)
   f. I could practice by joining a Toastmasters Club. (Maybe.)
   g. I could give up dealing with this issue entirely. (Unacceptable.)

3a. Identify a particular aspect of your own behavior that can be changed.
   a. I could become less nervous.
   b. I could train myself to become an excellent public speaker.

3b. Identify the effective thoughts that could possibly lead to that change.
   Effective thoughts 2, 6, 10, and 21 all seem appropriate and possible for me to employ.

ET 2—Approval: "I'm not really responsible for what an audience thinks of me when I make a presentation. All I need to do is approve of myself and the way I present."

ET 6—Experience: "If I want to present well, then I can do it. It doesn't pay to sit in the background and live my presentational life vicariously. Life is not a dress rehearsal."

ET 10—Help: "There's nothing to stop me from asking for help in making presentations. There's plenty of good training help to be had. All I need to do is ask for that help—and go for it."

ET 21—Risking: "While presenting is a risk, it is a risk well worth taking for the sake of forwarding my career."

4. Decide on a plan of action and write it down:
   a. I'll develop a line of effective thinking about my public speaking ability—and I'll use it.
   b. I'll volunteer to speak as often as possible.
   c. I'll practice, practice, practice.
   d. I'll take a short training course in presentational skills.
5. Move into action.
   a. Develop a line of effective thinking to overcome fear. (Completed. See below.)
   b. Volunteer to speak at every opportunity. (I'm doing that now.)
   c. Practice, practice, practice. (I'm doing that. Joined the Toastmasters, Inc., two weeks ago.)
   d. Take a presentational skills course. (I've enrolled and will attend first session on September 20th.)
6. Follow up and evaluate the effectiveness of the action taken.
   All this worked brilliantly. I delivered a "career-making" presentation. The corporate director attended and was extremely impressed. As a direct result of this strong presentation, I have been promoted to a key post in the special projects division of the company.

set you, not the actual giving of a presentation. So choose the thoughts that you've outlined for yourself. Pretend, next time you present, that you're enjoying yourself. And then you'll do fine."

Self-Coaching Case 3: Jack's Jealousy

Jack is very upset because the job promotion he expected to receive was given to Marion. The problem is his manager. Jack worked much harder than Marion did and feels that he was overlooked. His expectations were betrayed. Because the central figure in Jack's problem is his manager, self-coaching is necessarily very much in order. Here's how Jack proceeded, using the self-coaching worksheet shown in Figure 15-4.

Before, during, and after the time Jack took these actions, he engaged in a line of effective thinking that went something like this:

(text continued on p. 128)

Figure 15-4. Jack's six-step self-coaching worksheet.

1. Describe the issue in question below.
   I expected, and feel that I deserved, to be promoted to assistant manager. I was skipped over. I'm furious over being bypassed once again. I strongly feel that I deserved that promotion, not Marion. I've been here longer and I've worked harder. Besides, I was led to believe that if I did a good job at my present level, the assistant's job would be mine if it opened up. It opened up. I expected it. But when the announcement of the promotion came, it was given to Marion. Not only am I disappointed, I'm also very hurt.

2. Identify those externals (if any) that can be changed.
   a. I can try to speak to my boss about it and see if a change can be made in my favor. (Tried this, and I see that change is impossible.)
   b. I can quit this job and look for another one. (Not ready to take so drastic an action, at this point at least.)
   c. I can seek an assurance that I get the very next promotion that opens up. (This is the option that is left and the one I am going to take. If I do not get this assurance, I will move to seeking a promotion outside this company, not right now, but when I am ready.)

3a. Identify particular aspects of your own behavior that you can possibly change. Evaluate each and select those that seem most realistic.
   a. I can look like less of a patsy so that next time they'll be afraid to pass me by. (I figure that this is certainly an important thing to do.)
   b. I can do my present job even better and then become so attractive and visible in this work that other companies might try to woo me away. (Also an important thing to do.)
   c. I can accept this thing without getting any more upset than I already have. (Also an important thing to do.)
   d. I can leave and seek work elsewhere, right now. (Too drastic. Not at this point at least.)
   e. I can stay but get my résumé ready, and, when the time is ripe, leave for the job I think I deserve. (Not yet, but maybe soon.)
   f. I can get even more upset. (No value in this unless I want to force myself to up and leave very soon.)

3b. Identify the effective thoughts that will lead to the changes you have identified.
   The following thoughts in context might prove most useful in helping me to deal with this situation: numbers 7, 13, 14, 16, and 23.

> *ET 7—Facts:* "I can't change the fact that Marion got the promotion instead of me. I'll just have to deal with it."
>
> *ET 13—Justice:* "After all, there is no such thing as absolute justice. Life can sometimes be quite unfair. I'll have to work that through."
>
> *ET 14—Lovability:* "But even if I didn't get the promotion as promised, I'm still quite lovable. I'm in charge of feeling that way."
>
> *ET 16—Now:* "My life is made up only of nows. There's no value in wasting my time feeling jealous unless I use that jealousy creatively to accomplish something worthwhile."
>
> *ET 23—Uniqueness:* "I'm a very special human being marching to my own drummer. And sometimes that will be rewarded and sometimes not. Marion may have gotten the promotion, but that doesn't impinge one iota on the fact that I am very special, regardless of external circumstances."

4. Decide on a plan of action and write it down.
    I'm going to let the boss know where I stand. People have a tendency to treat you the way you teach them to treat you, and my boss is no exception to this rule. I'm also going to see to it that I am fully prepared and qualified when the chance for promotion comes again. Meanwhile, I'm getting my résumé in order and keeping Plan B (a job change) on the back burner.

5. Move into action. List a deadline for your planned action below.
    Let the boss know where I stand by May 22nd. Be prepared and qualified. Take an evening course. Enrolling for June 20th session at Piper U. Get résumé in shape by May 21 for possible job change. Hope not, but who knows?

6. Follow up and evaluate the effectiveness of the action taken.
    Did I get the next promotion? Yes, partly because, in relatively short order, I recovered from my disappointment. Using effective thinking, I quickly reestablished my equilibrium. That made moving into action much more rational, calculated, and smoothly executed. And my Plan A worked. I never had to resort to Plan B and use my updated résumé. Instead, I'm still with the same company and performing very well.

"I really should have known better. Too late now, but at least I'll know next time. I just shouldn't have staked so much of my emotional energy on the hope of getting that promotion. The truth is that in life, especially in business, you can't count 100 percent on variables outside yourself. Next time, I'll be less reasonable and more realistic—that is, if there ever is a 'next time.' It's about time that I came to terms with the fact that my business life can include a bit of loneliness in it. No one in this entire world knows exactly what it's like to be me. Got to come to terms with that. Got to let the pain of this setback sink in, then work it through as swiftly as possible. No sense dwelling on it and having it make me cynical. It's okay to be a bit skeptical. But cynical, no. There are just too many good things ahead for me to think cynically.

"Sure, I'm having a tough time knowing that I've been bypassed. Sure, I never expected to be treated so unfairly. Not in this place at least. I deserved that job, not Marion. But I've already tried bargaining with the boss, and he told me in no uncertain terms that the job was hers, not mine. Then I better get angry. [*And he does and lets his anger out on the racquet ball court, among other places.*] Now, I'd better get depressed." [*Doing that wasn't all that difficult. Feeling let down and disappointed was easy for him—especially in light of how badly he felt by virtue of losing out on the promotion.*]

Chapter 16

Starter File Of Effective Thoughts

In this book I have put a lot of emphasis on effective thinking, on the strength to be gained from deliberately choosing thoughts that will help you to turn around a tough situation. But this idea is new to most people, and even though they embrace it intellectually, they don't always know how to put it into action. I have found over the years from teaching effective thinking in many seminars in many industries that it helps to give some samples of effective thoughts. And that is what this chapter is about.

Here you will find a starter file of twenty-four thoughts that you might find effective in various circumstances. Used judiciously, they will serve you well for almost any situation that life might dish up. If you like any of them, feel free to use them as your own. Figure 16-1 lists the areas these thoughts cover. In the next section of the chapter, I show how effective thoughts come into play in various real-life contexts.

After you've looked through these, feel free to borrow, steal, or custom design any effective thought that comes to mind when you need one to suit a specific need. Invent some that suit your unique personality.

The Starter File of Effective Thoughts

1. *Aloneness.* You can sometimes get very close to others, but in actuality there will always be a part of you that is totally alone.

Figure 16-1. Areas covered by the twenty-four effective thoughts.

1. Aloneness	9. Guilt	17. Rejection
2. Approval	10. Help	18. Relationships
3. Body	11. Illness	19. Responsibility
4. Centering	12. Justice	20. Risking
5. Death	13. Lovability	21. Roles
6. Experience	14. Loving	22. Uniqueness
7. Facts	15. Now	23. Wholism
8. Feelings	16. Purpose	24. Worry

When you were born, the mold was broken and thrown away. There was never another person exactly like you on the face of this earth, and there never will be again. You were born alone and you will die alone. Others can get very close to you and you can get very close to others, but there will always be parts of you that no person but yourself can fully experience. The important thing to remember is not to run from aloneness but to allow yourself to experience it. You need not be lonely if you come to terms with your fundamental existential aloneness.

2. *Approval.* You cannot ever be fully responsible for how another person thinks about you.

Other people are responsible for their own thoughts—just as you are for yours. Although you can enjoy having others approve of you, you can never rely unfailingly on them to do so. If you act primarily for the sake of gaining the approval of others, you may very well end up pleasing no one. But if you act in a way that you yourself approve of, then at least one person will be pleased. And of course that one is you.

3. *Body.* Your body, as well as your mind, has intelligence.

It speaks to you—if you listen to it. It will tell you when it is enjoying something and when it is not. It has many other important messages for you. Learning from the "neck down" is as worthwhile as learning from the "neck up."

4. *Centering.* You cannot do everything.

You have to edit your existence, day by day. You have a center—if you allow yourself to experience it. Around your center you can integrate everything. You can discover what you are about, your own tastes, your own values. You can appreciate life qualitatively if not quantitatively, for you can only do one thing well at a given time.

5. *Death.* You are definitely going to die in a relatively short time.

Because it is estimated that the world as we know it has lasted for about fourteen billion years, even if you live a century or more, your lifetime is only a drop in the bucket. You will be in eternity for a long, long time. There will be no exception made in your case, no matter how well connected you are or become.

6. *Experience.* No one other than you can experience your life.

You can attempt to live vicariously through others by watching TV, daydreaming, reading novels, seeing movies, being a fan at sporting events or the like. However, it is quite possible for you to do many things firsthand in your own lifetime if you so chose and if you take appropriate risks.

7. *Facts.* You cannot change absolute facts.

All you can do about a fact is face it. However, if something is not a fact but an opinion, then you have the perfect right (and the capacity) to choose your own opinion. Because an opinion is a thought, you can learn how to choose effective opinions (thoughts)—that is, opinions that work for you instead of against you. "Correct" opinions (thoughts) are not necessarily effective opinions (thoughts).

8. *Feelings.* You own a marvelous sensory apparatus.

You can experience a tremendous amount in your lifetime, even in a moment or two, by fully employing the capacities of your senses. You can learn how to see more effectively, hear more clearly, smell more keenly, move more gracefully, and feel more sensitively. You can enrich your moment-by-moment existence at literally no cost.

9. *Guilt.* It makes no sense to wallow in guilt over what's already over.

What is done is definitely done. There is no going back. It makes sense to learn from your errors so as not to repeat them.

But nothing worthwhile is accomplished by self-blame over something that cannot be rectified. Self-responsibility is not the same as self-blame. You can make reparations (and should), but you cannot possibly go back in time.

10. *Help.* You can ask for help whenever you want or need it without being weak.

Perhaps you appear to be independent but are actually just afraid to ask for help, even though you may really need it. Embarrassment, fear of rejection, and social taboos often keep you locked into loneliness. Remember, it's perfectly all right for someone to say no to your request for help.

11. *Illness.* If you get ill, it will unfortunately be your own illness.

It will be your pain, and you will have to deal with it. You do have some powerful resources in your mind and body that you can employ, if you so choose, to help you deal effectively with such circumstances. Your thoughts especially can be powerful and useful in helping you to return to good health. It is your body and mind that will have to overcome the disease. Take care of them.

12. *Justice.* There is no such thing as absolute justice.

It is an abstract concept and you cannot always expect to get a fair shake. Sometimes evil is not punished, and good is not necessarily rewarded. Do not expect to be rewarded for your good works. Do what you do because you want to, because you believe it is right, not because of the justice you hope to receive.

13. *Lovability.* You can be lovable, but there is no guarantee that any other person, aside from yourself, will fully appreciate you for what you really are.

Lovable means "able to be loved." Most, if not all, children are born cuddly, small, and able to be loved. Even so, some are not loved. The fact that they are not loved does not mean they are not lovable. No one, lovable or not, can make another person love him. Chances are, however, that someone who feels lovable will eventually become loved. But there's no guarantee.

14. *Loving.* Loving involves listening to and caring for oth-

ers on their own terms without trying to superimpose your values upon them.

Loving involves an I-Thou attitude, empathy rather than sympathy, and personal openness. You cannot own the object of your love. Loving others adds clear purpose to your life.

15. *Now.* This present moment is all that you can ever be certain about.

It is yours to experience and to enjoy. It will soon be gone. You have only a limited number of present moments allocated to you. However, you can choose to use each one of them as you see fit. The past is gone forever. Your selective recall processes will distort your memory to protect your ego. The future is not assured in any way.

16. *Purpose.* It is much more productive to spend time searching for purpose and meaning than it is searching for happiness.

Happiness is a by-product, not an end in itself. If you search for it, it tends to elude you. Purpose and meaning, by contrast, are worthy ends, especially if your purpose is a passionate one. If someone has a *why* for existence, the *how* becomes secondary, yet readily discoverable. Purpose is achieved by loving something more than just yourself and also by reaching your goal.

17. *Rejection.* You cannot truly be rejected by someone who does not really care about you or know you.

A person who does not really care about you is incapable of listening effectively to you. And if he doesn't really listen to you, he can't get to know you, at least for what you really are. And if he does not know you for what you really are, then it's not you he is actually rejecting but rather his illusion of you. Therefore, it is foolish to take much so-called personal rejection personally or seriously.

18. *Relationships.* All interpersonal relationships are in actuality quite conditional—value given for value received.

This becomes clearer in long-term relationships. Even your closest friend or your spouse accepts you on a conditional basis. If, for example, you decide to "cheat" on this friend or on your spouse, the character of the relationship is bound to change.

There is a hierarchy in one's relationships; you value some more than you do others.

19. *Responsibility.* You are fully responsible for yourself and your actions.

Actually, you are responsible for yourself and your actions whether you acknowledge it or not. No one else is ever responsible for what you think or feel. You are, in a very real sense, in charge of your own destiny, whether you want to be or not.

20. *Risking.* You can make life exciting and adventurous by intelligent risk taking.

Effective risk-taking behavior can be learned and applied. If you take no risks, you won't suffer too much. But you won't accomplish very much either. Nor will you have much fun. You should take effective risks often to avoid lethargy and dullness.

21. *Roles.* In everyday life you are often required to play various roles.

There is a significant distinction between playing a role and doing a job. Playing the role of manager, for example, can be quite different from the act of managing. Playing roles is often necessary, but role-playing by definition is never really a very serious business. Doing a job is almost always serious business. One can often do both well, but it is important to be aware of the considerable differences between the two. Never confuse the roles you play with who you really are.

22. *Uniqueness.* There is a unique rhythm inside you.

It is a rhythm all your own that you dance to or march to as you wish. No one else can feel it. You are not crazy just because others don't hear this music. They have their own, if they will just listen for it.

23. *Wholism.* You are all of one piece.

Your mind, body, and spirit are one. Although, in a basic sense, your thoughts, feelings, and behavior are all of one piece too, it is useful to remember that your thoughts are the "key," your feelings are "where you really live," and your behavior is that small part of you that "goes public."

24. *Worry.* There is absolutely no value in ordinary worry.

You can turn your problems into projects, and then you will not have worries. You might have due concern, but not worry.

Due concern is creative worry. But *ordinary worry* implies spinning your wheels unnecessarily. *Concern* suggests taking proper steps, one at a time. But ordinary worry is a complete waste of valuable time in every way. It serves no valid function whatsoever.

Effective Thoughts in Specific Contexts

In Figure 16-2, you will find a summary list of thirty-two situations that are common either in business or in everyday life. In every case, the situation could be ameliorated by the choice of effective thoughts. In the following paragraphs, I show you some of the typical defective, self-defeating thoughts that often come up in each of these situations and then contrast them with effective thoughts applicable to the same context. There's a good chance that something here will help you with a problem you're having right now.

Substituting Effective for Defective Thoughts

1. Blaming on the job

Defective thought: "I'm not really responsible for my own job performance. Outside circumstances and forces make me perform in certain ways."

Effective thought: (helps in avoiding being irresponsible about one's own job performance) "The one thing that I truly own is me. I accept and enjoy full responsibility for my own on-the-job performance. I keep an eye on myself, being self-conscious to a fault. I've noticed that wherever I go, there I am."

2. Giving too much credit to luck on the job

Defective thought: "Oh, look how I stumbled upon this amazing solution. I'm so lucky."

Effective thought: (helps in overcoming embarrassment caused by success or good fortune on the job) "Oh, look how I

Figure 16-2. Thirty-two situations that call for effective thoughts.

1. Blaming on the job
2. Giving too much credit to luck on the job
3. Being preoccupied with the past
4. Always deferring the now, "someday, I'm gonna" on the job
5. Counting on factors outside oneself on the job
6. Failing to have an alternative plan on the job
7. Failure on the job
8. Avoiding procrastination
9. Being too unrealistic about the job
10. Being possessed by one's possessions
11. Waiting for "the next life" before enjoying oneself
12. Feeling too much loneliness on the job
13. Worrying too much about how one will be remembered after death
14. Failing to gain closure on or to work through a loss rapidly enough
15. Failing to take sufficient credit for a job well done
16. Living one's life too vicariously
17. Excessive worry on the job
18. Excessive fear on the job
19. Being too needy
20. Improving relationships on and off the job
21. Improving the quality of one's marriage
22. Being a poor listener
23. Not being sufficiently prepared for retirement
24. Being treated unjustly on or off the job
25. Taking a job title too seriously
26. Feeling untalented
27. Feeling stupid
28. Fearing to take risks on and off the job
29. Feeling trapped by one's job
30. Feeling afraid to share
31. Feeling nervous on the job
32. Fouling up on the job

stumbled upon this amazing solution. I apparently set my-self so that these things often happen."

3. Being preoccupied with the past

Defective thought: "The job in the good old days, those were the days, my friend."

Effective thought: (helps in keeping focused on the joys of work today and the promises of tomorrow) "Today's job is an exciting job, my friend. Yesterday is already distorted by selective memory. And yesterday is gone forever."

4. Always deferring the now, "someday, I'm gonna" on the job

Defective thought: "I've got plenty of plans for my job tomorrow. Someday I'll . . ."

Effective thought: (helps in making the most of every moment on the job) "Today is still the day, my friend. Tomorrow is at best uncertain and in fact may never come. Today on this job is for sure."

5. Counting on factors outside oneself on the job

Defective thought: "I'm counting on stability. My family, my friends, my job, my boss . . ."

Effective thought: (helps in sustaining self-reliance on and off the job) "The only thing I can absolutely count on is change. I can handle change without too much difficulty."

6. Failing to have an alternative plan on the job

Defective thought: "I've worked hard on this job plan and I've got to see it through, no matter what."

Effective thought: (fosters flexibility on the job when that becomes necessary) "I've worked hard on this job plan. But I've included in it several alternative plans, a plan B and even a plan C, and I'm prepared to table all of them if something more appropriate becomes necessary."

7. Failure on the job

Defective thought: "The project bombed and I'm crushed. I've failed at it. I'm a failure.

Effective thought: (helps in seeing a temporary failure on the job as a learning opportunity) "An aspect of the job failed this time; but what can I take from this experience to help me succeed if I choose to try again? The project might have failed, but not me. After all, I'm not the project."

8. Avoiding procrastination

Defective thought: "I'll try."

Effective thought: "I will."

9. Being too unrealistic about the job

Defective thought: "Somehow, some way, things on this job will come out alright. Something is bound to turn up to help my dream come true. I may even be whisked into a better situation here or at some other company."

Effective thought: (helps in gaining a down-to-earth perspective on the job) "There's really no special magic working for me. If I seriously want something better to happen on this job, I've got to set in motion things and forces to make it happen. However, all the vicissitudes that affect other people can happen to me too—sickness, winning the lottery if I take a chance, getting hurt. . . ."

10. Being possessed by one's possessions

Defective thought: "I enjoy and feel proud that I own this workstation, my home, this gorgeous coat, this brooch, this business firm. I know there are many people who are jealous of me and who would like to take them away. But I'm keeping my eye on all the things that I own."

Effective thought: (helps in preventing being owned by one's possessions on and off the job) "I travel light. I sometimes enjoy using things. Although I possess legal title to some of these things, I don't feel that I own them. I think of the use of things, the experiencing of things, but I realize that my use of them is strictly pro tem. After all, I don't want these things to restrict my flexibility and spontaneity. When I'm away from them, let others use them. In essence, the way I look at it, every material possession, even the job I have, is merely rented, and I like it that way. I'm not going to be buried with them. I'll leave that to King Tut."

11. Waiting for "the next life" before enjoying oneself

Defective thought: "Maybe I'll do better on the job I have in the next life."

Effective thought: (helps in overcoming procrastination) "This life is it. This is the job I have in hand. If there's another, of course I'll accept it as a bonus, but I'll be damned if I'll count on it."

12. Feeling too much loneliness on the job

Defective thought: "I can't stand being alone. I need others around me. If I'm alone too long, I get very sad and lonely."

Effective thought: (helps in coming to terms with the loneliness that is associated with moving up the organizational pyramid) "I often enjoy working alone. I enjoy being close to others when this happens, but I realize that in the final analysis I was born alone, live essentially alone, and eventually will die alone. I can live and work alone without feeling lonely.

13. Worrying too much about how one will be remembered after death

Defective thought: "After I pass away I want to be remembered and well thought of."

Effective thought: (helps in handling the pressure that often accompanies maintaining a professional reputation) "When I die, that's it. What others think of me then won't bring me back. Those who really want to know me can do so right now. How anyone chooses to remember me doesn't interest me one iota."

14. Failing to gain closure on or to work through a loss rapidly enough

Defective thought: "Why did I lose that big sale? What bad luck I'm having. Oh, oh. What a rotten deal I've gotten. Damn. Poor me."

Effective thought: (helps in recovering quickly from an on-the-job setback) "I lost the sale. That really hurts. What I've got to do now is think, and pause and work this through rapidly and then see how I can turn this lost sale into something worthwhile."

15. Failing to take sufficient credit for a job well done

Defective thought: "I didn't really write [build, create, accomplish] this. I got so much wonderful help from so many others."

Effective thought: (helps in developing greater self-esteem) "I did that. Others may have offered advice and suggestions and even a helping hand. But in the final analysis, it would never have come off it if hadn't been for my initiative and risk taking."

16. Living one's life too vicariously

Defective thought: "I'm living for my children's future. I'm hanging in there for the day when they. . . ."

Effective thought: (helps in taking on-the-job risks now) "I'm mainly living my own life. After all, this is my one and only chance to live it, as far as I know, with any degree of certainty."

17. Excessive worry on the job

Defective thought: "I worry, worry, worry, and worry still more."

Effective thought: (helps in reducing unnecessary stress) "I have due concern, due concern, and no more than due concern."

18. Excessive fear on the job

Defective thought: "This frightens me and that's a fact."

Effective thought: (helps in enabling you to face the facts of life) "It is thinking I'm afraid that frightens me, and that's a fact."

19. Being too needy

Defective thought: "I absolutely must have her support."

Effective thought: (helps in being more relaxed) "I would prefer it if she offered a bit of help."

20. Improving relationships on and off the job

Defective thought: "All relationships are fair and equal."

Effective thought: (helps in avoiding the attempt to be all things to all people) "There's usually a pecking order governing human relationships, but they're not always based upon value given for value received."

21. Improving the quality of one's marriage

Defective thought: "Marriage involves two half persons fused into a whole."

Effective thought: (helps in developing a deeper and more lasting relationship that serves as a support for on-the-job performance) "Two unique people plus a marriage equal three."

22. Being a poor listener

Defective thought: "I already know what my teammate is trying to say, so I'll just pretend that I'm listening to his ideas. Then later, I'll tell him what I think."

Effective thought: (helps in one's efforts to become a more caring person on and off the job) "My teammate is special and unique, one of a kind. I'm going to care for and listen to him on his own terms. I expect to get closer to him so that I can genuinely understand and appreciate his feelings on this matter."

23. Not being sufficiently prepared for retirement

Defective thought: "When I retire, I'd better take up a hobby or something interesting."

Effective thought: (helps to keep you from postponing having an interesting life) "I'd better take up something really interesting now, something meaningful that can carry me right through retirement. In fact, I'll never retire. I'll just enter a new phase of an exciting life."

24. Being treated unjustly on or off the job

Defective thought: "That so-and-so will someday get punished by the fates. I don't know what it will be, but justice will triumph."

Effective thought: (helps in coping successfully with some kinds of unfairness) "That guy won't necessarily get his. This isn't the way I'd like the world to work, but it often does operate that way. Justice doesn't always triumph. I've learned to live with this and not to use up my limited time and energy wishing for justice—at least for me in this lifetime."

25. Taking a job title too seriously

Defective thought: "I'm a shipping clerk."

Effective thought: (helps to separate substance from form) "I ship important goods to important people."

Defective thought: "I'm a doctor."

Effective thought: "I work at healing people."

26. Feeling untalented

Defective thought: "I have no special talent for doing this job."

Effective thought: (helps in creating a positive self-fulfilling prophecy) "I am a creative and talented performer on this job."

27. Feeling stupid

Defective thought: "I'm not too bright when it comes to this."

Effective thought: (helps in engendering self-confidence) "I can understand practically anything. I'm in no great rush. I have my own style and rhythm for learning. It may take me a little longer than it does the next fellow. But I assure you that I can understand practically anything, given sufficient time. That's assuming, of course, that it is something I really want to learn."

28. Fearing to take risks on and off the job

Defective thought: "I like to play it safe. An old and familiar job, trustworthy friends, famous brands, a clear road map on safe, major highways—these are what I need. I like to know well in advance what to expect. I'm not one for big surprises."

Effective thought: (helps in becoming more adventurous) "I enjoy getting off the beaten path once in a while. I learn and discover when I take chances. I like adventure, excitement, and taking risks. I enjoy new jobs, new relationships, loving, leaving, making money, expressing what I feel, sometimes failing, and changing."

29. Feeling trapped by one's job

Defective thought: "I get so caught up in having to do this and that. I feel I have no choice. Sometimes I feel so pressured and confined that I want to scream."

Effective thought: (helps make possible a greater sense of freedom on the job) "I have ordered my priorities and clarified my values. I know how to and do edit each day. I always have thought choices and I know that suffering is optional. I make sure to take time each day to enjoy certain aspects of my relatively short life."

30. Feeling afraid to share

Defective thought: "I think that if people ever found out what I'm really like, my world would fall apart. I'm a very private person."

Effective thought: (helps in becoming more open) "I enjoy my privacy, but, frankly, I don't mind sharing any aspect of myself whatsoever if others are really interested. I don't think most people really concern themselves with me that much. They're usually preoccupied with themselves. But I'm generally quite open because I know that openness can never harm me in the long run."

31. Feeling nervous on the job

Defective thought: "Things that go on in this crazy office really make me nervous."

Effective thought: (helps in sustaining a sense of inner calm when others are feeling pressure) "If I ever get nervous, I say to myself, 'You're making yourself nervous.' Then I say, 'Are you enjoying or valuing being nervous?' Then I usually answer, 'No, I am not enjoying being nervous.' Next I say, 'Stop choosing thoughts that are making you nervous and start choosing thoughts that make you calm.' Then I follow my instructions to the letter and end up very calm."

32. Fouling up on the job

Defective thought: "I fouled up. I'm just no good. I should never have tried to do this task. I'll never be able to get back on schedule."

Effective thought: (helps in becoming more decisive) "I fouled up. But at least I really enjoyed myself letting go of my plan for once. Wow, I really fouled up! But that's OK. I'm back on schedule now as of this very moment. Feels good to be back on course."

And if nothing here seems to work for you in a given situation, make up your own effective thoughts. Use the following worksheet.

YOUR OWN LIST OF EFFECTIVE THOUGHTS

When you are ready, jot down the thoughts that, from time to time, you have found to be useful and effective for you in various situations. Keep this list up to date. Delete those that cease to appeal to you.

_____

_____

_____

_____

_____

_____

_____

_____

_____

_____

_____

_____

_____

_____

_____

_____

_____

_____

_____

_____

_____

Part V

Reaching the Peak Performance Zone: A Review

Let's briefly review the main steps for creating peak performance motivation and, ultimately, a peak performance zone.

1. You must commit yourself to using the three-step Creating PPM system as soon as possible. In that you've practically finished this book, I trust that you've already done this.

2. You first embark upon steps 1 and 2 of the system, teaching people how to take total self-responsibility and leading them to a recognition of sufficient WIIFMs that they will *want* to perform at peak.

3. You provide those who qualify with peak performance mentoring—and then watch their smoke. The peak performance zone will fall automatically into place.

4. Once the zone is operational, you monitor the zone and make yourself available to your peak performers as a continuing helper—if called upon. Otherwise, you prudently stay out of the way.

5. You must consistently draw upon your own effective thoughts and stay totally responsible for your own performance as a manager. Choose thoughts that make you a peak performance

manager. You must keep yourself in great psychological and physical shape so that you can perform at your very best and set the proper example for your people.

Finally, I'd like you to read a story about a peak performance manager—Vincent—and one of his staff members, Trent. Vincent is head of production at a microchip manufacturing company in Massachusetts, and one day Trent was assigned to his team. Vincent took a substandard performer and turned him into a self-responsible, self-motivated peak performer. In his own words, here's how he did it:

> "I had this fellow, Trent, put on my team. He wasn't the kind of worker I would have hired, but I had no choice in the matter. In no time I could see why he wasn't working up to par. He was a 'blamer'—always blaming other people when things didn't work right. He was definitely a problem worker. So I decided that instead of keeping him as a problem, I'd convert him into a peak performance project.
>
> "Trent's job was to arrange various computer parts in a special sequence on the assembly bench. But he was very careless. He sometimes mixed up the sequence of the computer parts layout on the bench. And this tied up the next step in the sequence.
>
> "Here's what I did. I called him aside and I told him in no uncertain terms that his work was way under par and totally unacceptable. I asked him what he proposed to do about it. 'I'm going to try harder,' he said. *Try harder.* A meaningless phrase if ever I heard one.
>
> "I told him, 'No, Trent, trying harder isn't going to do it. I want you to enroll in my mandatory self-responsibility seminar. I'm going to teach you how to take full charge of all your own performances and show you how to become one of the best producers in our department.'
>
> "He showed up. Actually, he didn't have all that much choice. Anyway, I taught him all about thought choosing, effective thinking, the A-B-Cs of choosing, and all that. He took to the training. In fact, he was a very good student. I was proud of him.
>
> "And then I offered to mentor him, to take him to the top in his field if he wanted to learn how. He took me up on my

offer. In one of our mentoring/counseling talks I found out that Trent had lots of hardship in his past. Without going into detail, it was the fact that his mother apparently never gave him much credit for anything, even when he did well in school. Once he got a prize for his extra work in shop—and his family said nothing.

"It didn't take genius on either of our parts to figure out that Trent might be very responsive to praise. That was his WIIFM. So I used praise whenever possible; any time I found him doing something good, I quickly praised him. His work improved bit by bit each day. Later in the year, I got the company to present Trent with an engraved plaque noting the company's appreciation for his good effort. And we all applauded him. The whole department.

"A few weeks after this little awards ceremony, I noticed that my 'atta boys' and all my other forms of praise, recognition, and appreciation were losing some of their effectiveness. My praise was wearing a bit thin. WIIFMs, like anything else, are subject to the law of diminishing returns. So I immediately went back to my WIIFM drawing board. What could we, Trent and I, use now to move him upward? We met and figured out that "a very special and important assignment" had a great deal of appeal to him. He wanted to try, all on his own, to develop a plan for expediting all our computer production. He took to it like a duck to water. He even surprised himself by systematically conducting a very intensive production efficiency study. It took him three weeks, and after he finished it he said he'd like to expedite the implementation of his new design. He showed me his completed report and I was very impressed. He figured out a way for us to actually triple our production output, and with no additions to the work force.

"Turns out that Trent's plan worked wonders. Of course, it hasn't all been a bed of roses. He still comes to me now and then for a bit of counseling and coaching. But he's a peak performer now—and I think I had something to do with it."

Chapter 17
Highlights

My final chapter consists of sixteen peak performance reminders. Look at them periodically to keep yourself on your peak performance managerial track; turn back to specific chapters for further details, as needed.

Reminder 1

The Creating PPM system consists of three uncomplicated steps:

1. Take total self-responsibility for all your own job performances. Then model that quality and teach your direct reports how to do the same thing.
2. Make available to each of your direct reports some very good reasons for wanting to perform at peak.
3. Mentor (which includes counseling and coaching) your direct reports to the point where they are clearly performing at peak. After that, stay out of their way.

Reminder 2

The consistent, enduring peak performer aims to:

▲ Take total responsibility for all his own job performances
▲ Be an *effective*, but not necessarily a *positive*, thinker
▲ Find sufficient reason to *want* to perform at peak
▲ Be self-motivated
▲ Share generously and, hence, be an excellent team player

▲ Seek peak performance mentoring when necessary
▲ Have a rich and satisfying personal *and* professional life

Reminder 3

Certain traits of peak performance managers are what distinguish them from the rest of the pack. The peak performance manager:

▲ Learns all he can about how to motivate peak performance.
▲ Takes, models, and teaches total self-responsibility for one's own performance.
▲ Is inner-directed.
▲ Helps his people get a fair share of the action.
▲ Is self-motivated.
▲ Avails his people of sufficient reasons to want to excel.
▲ Understands the basics of self-motivation.
▲ Sees himself in a service function dedicated to helping each of his performers perform at peak.
▲ Offers peak performance mentoring exclusively to his qualified probable peak performers, by performer request only.
▲ Stays out of the way of his peak performers unless his help is sought.
▲ Enjoys his managerial life in the peak performance zone.

Reminder 4

To be a peak performance manager:

Do: see yourself as a helper to your peak performers and as a helper to and motivator of your standard performers. Peak performance managers tend to see themselves as equal partners with their performers, not as their "superiors."

Don't: seriously see yourself as a "boss" or as a "superior" to your direct reports.

Do: take total, 100 percent responsibility for your thoughts, feelings, and performance.

Don't: blame others or external events for your thoughts, feelings, and performance.

Do: believe that all people are motivated by self-interest.

Don't: believe that people act against their own self-interests if they know better.

Do: believe that the interests of the company and the interests of its workers can be highly compatible and complementary and know how to combine these two self-interests into a successful life in the peak performance zone.

Don't: believe that the interests of the company and the interests of its workers must be mutually exclusive.

Do: know how to listen to feelings.

Don't: believe that a worker's feelings are of little importance.

Do: everything in your power to see to it that your standard and substandard performers learn how to take total self-responsibility.

Don't: permit or condone blaming or buck passing by anyone for any reason.

Do: everything in your power to sustain the level of self-responsibility that your peak performers attain.

Don't: allow your peak performers to believe that they are not in charge of their own behavior.

Do: your best to provide a fair share of the action to your workers.

Don't: keep all the action for yourself.

Do: know how to successfully employ a variety of peak performance motivational strategies, especially peak performance mentoring.

Don't: stop learning all you can about how to motivate yourself and others to higher and higher levels of peak performance.

Do: know how to create, enjoy, and sustain a highly productive, profitable, and satisfying life in the peak performance zone.

Don't: intend ever to permit yourself to slip back into being a substandard or standard manager.

Reminder 5

Take the self-responsibility test (in Chapter 5) from time to time to see how you're doing and maintaining your focus.

Reminder 6

Use the self-responsibility imperative often: "Whenever necessary, pause and think, and then choose effective thoughts."

"Whenever Necessary": Peak performers have the goal of having richly satisfying lives. And since this goal is always at the back of their minds, they are particularly sensitive to those times when the feelings they are experiencing are not in keeping with this fundamental commitment.

"Pause and Think": Pausing and thinking is a crucial part of the self-responsibility sentence. One excellent use of "pausing" is to break the pattern of a defective mind-set. It's your basic mind-set that determines what you see in a given situation.

"Then Choose Effective Thoughts": All self-responsible, effective thinkers believe that they have the power to choose any thought that they need at any time and in any place. And so they consciously choose effective thoughts—thoughts that help them attain their goals—rather than the defective thoughts that work against them.

Reminder 7

If deliberate thought choosing doesn't work in a given instance (and sometimes it doesn't), then use the A-B-C approach:

Plan A—the Aggravation Technique
Plan B—the Branding Tactic
Plan C—the Closure Process

These are used only when choosing at a conscious level is difficult. They make use of your subconscious.

The Aggravation Technique is based on the well-established psychological principle of *implosion*. Through implosion, the patient deliberately makes things worse (aggravating them) before they get better.

The Branding Tactic is a quick and easy self-hypnosis strategy that *brands* effective thoughts deeply into your subconscious. Remember the exercise you did with the word *green*.

The Closure Process involves "working through," or resolving, unfinished business from your past that is producing self-defeating thoughts. When it is extremely difficult to choose effective thoughts over defective ones, even after you've tried and tried, you may need to use the Closure Process.

Reminder 8

Remember the WIIFM principle: "All persons (peak performers and others as well) are motivated, at bottom, by self-interest." Put bluntly, people inevitably ask themselves "What's in it for me?" Even you. A self-responsible performer can find a sufficient reason to excel if there's a WIIFM or two (or more) to strike the proper sensitive nerve.

Reminder 9

Remind yourself of the kinds of motivations that are likely to be intrinsic:

- ▲ Enjoyment of the work itself
- ▲ Having a "piece of the action"—sharing visions, missions, leadership, authority, and responsibility
- ▲ Pride in performing excellently
- ▲ Proving some secret point to oneself

▲ Achievement of a deep-seated value (such as helping another person)
▲ Strong belief in the importance of the work one is doing
▲ The excitement and pleasure of a challenge
▲ Desire to exceed one's previous level of job performance
▲ Receipt of "psychic" (as opposed to material) income

Reminder 10

Some of the following WIIFMs are likely to motivate your probable peak performers:

Trusting and being trusted
A mutual mission
TQM
Benchmarking
Quality circles
A mutual, measurable objective
A quality work life
More money
Psychic income

Reminder 11

Remember to mentor people with high potential for peak performance. Peak performance mentoring includes taking a very special interest in your performer, showing him the ropes, helping him weather company politics, borrowing from your wisdom and experience. Your mentoring will also include client-centered counseling and coaching. But remember, your mentoring is offered to, never superimposed upon, one of your peak performers. Also remember that mentoring is only available to those performers who have qualified by becoming self-responsible probable peak performers.

Reminder 12

The five steps for client-centered counseling are:

1. Before the first session, complete a precounseling empathy form.

2. Establish rapport. Assure the counselee that what you are about to discuss is confidential. Set a specific time frame (usually no more than forty minutes) for the session.
3. Help your counselee to identify and clarify an area of focus for the session.
4. Listen deeply and empathetically, but refrain from giving any advice. Don't forget that one of your main duties is to develop or sustain a self-responsible performer. Therefore, remain as nonjudgmental as you possibly can.
5. Close the session within the time allotted. Suggest a follow-up session if appropriate. Give some kind of "psychological homework."

Reminder 13

Remember the six steps of peak performance coaching:

1. Help the coachee to identify and clarify the nature of the specific issue.
2. Help the coachee to identify those externals (if any) of the situation that can be changed.
3. Help the coachee to identify (a) a particular aspect of his or her own behavior that can be changed, and (b) the effective thoughts that will lead to that behavior change.
4. Help the coachee to develop and decide upon a plan of action.
5. Help the coachee to move into action.
6. Follow up and evaluate the effectiveness of the action taken.

Help your mentorees use the Six-Step Coaching Worksheet, on which they write down in their own words their thoughts about the six steps.

During the coaching session, remind your coachee to make a simultaneous two-pronged attack upon the issue in question: (1) Attack the disturbing issue *attitudinally* with effective thoughts, and (2) *practically* through concrete actions and steps.

Reminder 14

Refer frequently to Chapter 16 for the list of twenty-four effective thought areas and for the list of thirty-two real-life situations in which effective thinking would be useful.

Reminder 15

Remember the four zones that apply to every worker, manager, team, company, or organization:

1. The no performance zone
2. The low performance zone
3. The moderate performance zone
4. The peak performance zone.

The no performance zone organization is obviously doomed to fail. The low performance zone organization needs all the help it can get. The moderate performance zone organization can manage to just get by, if it is lucky.

But the peak performance zone organization reflects the best place to be for any worker, team, or division. Aim to bring your entire group into the peak performance zone.

Reminder 16

Visualize frequently life in the peak performance zone. Now and then reexperience the visualization exercise in Chapter 4.

And that's it. Here's to continuing self-responsibility. And to many more sufficient reasons for you to want to perform at your managerial best. And to the mentoring and learning that you yourself continue to seek—in the form of ideas, books, and people you respect. And here's to the management profession and our important work of helping people to do their best. Finally, here's to many more exciting and productive years in your own personal peak performance zone.

Index